A MANUAL OF BASIC

WILDERNESS

SURVIVOR'S GUIDE

SURVIVAL TECHNIQUES

for

SCOUTS, HUNTERS, CAMPERS, HIKERS, CANOEISTS, PILOTS, AND ALL OTHERS UNPREPARED TO MEET THE CHALLENGE.

Stan Hamper

SCHROEDER PUBLISHING CO., INC.

Originally published in 1963 as *Wilderness Survival*, the manuscript was expanded by the author in the late 1970s and revised by his widow for publication as *Wilderness Survivor's Guide*.

This book should be used neither as a complete outdoor reference nor an exclusive skills textbook. The information here may be helpful to campers, hunters, hikers, and other outdoor enthusiasts but neither the late author's family nor the publisher can be held liable or responsible for any personal harm or equipment damage incurred by the book's users.

Cover design by Beth Summers

Book design by Mary Ann Hudson

Illustrations by Stan Hamper

Schroeder Publishing Inc.
P.O. Box 3009
Paducah, Kentucky 42002-3009

www.collectorbooks.com

Copyright © 1963 Stan Hamper
2001 Revised Edition, Margaret Hamper

CONTENTS

DEDICATION

The Boy Scouts of America is by far the most dynamic boys' organization in the world. Judging by the number of adults who participate in the program as leaders, the program is also an important adult avocation.

My twenty-five years of affiliation with the Scouting program have been invaluable and rewarding both as a boy and as an adult.

It is with pleasure that I dedicate this book to all Scouts and Scouters in the hope that it will add much to their enjoyment of the out-of-doors in keeping with the high ideals of self reliance — a prime purpose of Scouting.

ABOUT THE AUTHOR

Stan Hamper enjoyed a life filled with many interests. As a young boy in the Scouting program he earned the rank of Eagle Scout with Silver Palm and as an adult was the recipient of the Silver Beaver. A WW II Navy veteran, he saw service in the Atlantic, Mediterranean, and Pacific theaters. After service he trained as an archaeologist with three years' work in the Southwest. Active in research and development engineering, he served as chief engineer for several corporations. His hobbies included watercolor portraiture, pen and ink, wood carving, and model design and building, as well as collecting early American lighting.

He was founding director of the Southwestern Michigan College Museum 1981 – 1992. After retiring, he continued his interest in research and writing and served as volunteer curator for the National Heddon Museum from 1995 until his death on October 2, 1998.

Hamper's first book, *Wilderness Survival,* written in 1963, was sold nationally and used as a textbook by the National Camping Association and the Colorado Outward Bound School. The book was also widely used by Scout groups, canoe outfitters, and walkers on the Appalachian Trail.

Historical Reflections of Cass County, compiled for the Cass County Historical Commission in 1981, Hamper's first book on area history, was primarily a reference about architecturally and historically significant homes in Cass County, Michigan.

A third book, *Waterpowered Mills in Cass County,* published in 1993, pointed out the significance of water power in that area's development. *Dowagiac Stories – Windows to the Past,* Volumes I and II, published in 1996 and 1998, highlight that community's treasured tales.

Lighting Devices and Accessories of the 17th – 19th Centuries was published posthumously in 2001 by Hamper's widow, Margaret L. Hamper. *Wilderness Survivor's Guide* is Margaret's most recent publishing project. In acknowledging Margaret's support, advice, and encouragement, Hamper inscribed her copy of *Dowagiac Stories,* Vol. I: To Margaret: for dotting the i's, crossing the t's with patience and love.

INTRODUCTION

The tremendous increase in the sales of fishing, boating, camping and hunting equipment over the last few years is indicative of the rapid increase in participation in these activities. It is, therefore, a wonder that there are still areas in North America that can be regarded as wilderness. Luckily, a few areas remain for those of us that appreciate getting away once in a while to enjoy the out-of-doors, free of unattended camp fires, scarred birch trees, used facial tissue, bullet-riddled road signs, and cans of all sizes, shapes, and descriptions. These still pristine areas are scattered over all of North America — east, west, north, and south. Each presents a different type of wilderness experience.

Unfortunately, many who venture forth are not equipped for such junkets. Four or five hundred dollars worth of the finest equipment does not certify the owner as an expert nor does it assure the success or safety of any trip he might take.

Any amateur should include some basic wilderness lore training as a prerequisite to any planned excursion. Since being hopelessly lost for 5 or 6 days — cold, wet, hungry, and thirsty — will take the starch out of even the strong at heart.

In compiling *Wilderness Survival*, I kept in mind that "a picture is worth a thousand words." Detailed drawings, some explaining techniques step by step, in my opinion, present the most readable and understandable survival manual.

I offer the following pages as a guide in hopes that you will remember some of what you read regarding the basic concepts of survival. If you will retain enough to give you a head start, whether lost, stranded or simply out enjoying what nature has to offer, I feel my offerings are worthwhile.

During the years between the original edition of *Wilderness Survival* in 1963 and the final revision to the first edition in 1975, millions of acres of wilderness here and abroad were destroyed. Since 1975 the rate of destruction has increased even more drastically. More and more roads have made remote areas more and more accessible. Resorts, housing developments, factories, pollution from acid rain, strip mining, and overcutting of forest areas have added to a continuing and generally downward spiral toward eventual ecological disaster.

In this revised and enlarged edition of a volume written originally for the individual as a training manual, the text shifts its emphasis to promoting survival of the wilderness itself. If readers using this manual become aware of the wonders of nature and how those wonders relate to their personal survival, perhaps that knowledge will help to save, maintain, and improve the wilderness areas we now have and increase their number and variety.

ORIENTATION
ON BECOMING LOST OR STRANDED

Common sense and self reliance will be your staunch allies when stranded in a wilderness area providing you allow them time to shift into high gear. If fear takes over first, your ability to react logically to the situation will be seriously hampered. Incidents of becoming lost or stranded are legion. Probably many of you are aware of examples of such experiences.

Several years ago a group of businessmen drove to a Canadian resort for a week of fishing. One morning they hired a bush pilot to fly them to a remote lake where fishing was excellent. Arriving early, they planned to fish for five or six hours after which the plane was to return and pick them up. The appointed hour for the return flight came and went. Eventually, night closed in with no signs of their transportation. It was obvious that the men were stranded at least until morning.

Although a fire was eventually kindled, the men stood most of the night since sitting near the fire overheated their front sides while the "back forty" froze. A drop in temperature and a light rain mixed with snow put an "icing on the cake." They had no food, were not dressed for conditions, and had no shelter. Luckily the plane arrived next morning at which time the pilot explained that he had been called out early the previous afternoon to help in the search for a group of lost fisherman — a rather ironic set of circumstances.

It is easy for the "arm chair Dan'l Boone" to chuckle, cozy up to the fireplace, sip his coffee, and analyze the obvious mistakes the men made.

1. *Water.* Should be no problem since a whole lake of good water was only a few paces away. Most usually water in lakes in the far north is pure enough for drinking without boiling, providing no resorts are close by.

2. *Shelter.* There were certainly enough pine trees nearby to afford material to make many shelters — certainly enough to provide one large enough to accommodate four men. Their reels of fish line offered more than enough line for lashing. Pine boughs could also have been used to make good ground insulators for sitting and sleeping.

3. *Fire.* There should have been no problem in kindling. Efficiency and usefulness could have been improved if a reflector had been built.

4. *Food.* There were more fish available than could have been eaten in a week! They could have been cleaned and cooked on a stick, wrapped in mud and baked, planked and pegged, or stripped and smoked. It also seems probable that edible plants could have been located, water lily tubers or cattails for example, since they usually grow in abundance in most lakes. Birch twigs boiled in water or birch sap added to water would also have produced a very palatable hot drink.

Unfortunately, being able to analyze the mistakes others have made will not necessarily mean that you would react logically in a similar situation. When the first indications of panic roll over you, do something quick! Pick out a target and throw stones, go for a swim, soak your head or sit quietly on a rock and yell like a banshee. If you are with others, sit down quietly and discuss the situation. Take stock of the equipment you have and discuss the possible uses of each item. A surprising number of good ideas can result from such a discussion. Remember — clawing your way through the tall timber will do little to improve your position.

Don't turn an incident into a tragedy!

MAP ORIENTATION

 Before making any trip into unknown or unfamiliar territory, acquaint yourself with available maps. United States Geodetic Survey maps are available for most areas although they cannot always be presumed to be current and/or accurate.

Sketch proposed routes and take note of outstanding landmarks, cabins, trails, streams, portages, etc. Orient these features in relation to the direction of North. During your trip, consult your map often and note any additional points of reference or map discrepancies. The time spent will be invaluable since your unconscious assimilation of information will help you if you do become involved in an "incident."

EMERGENCY ORIENTATION

Without the aid of a compass, North can still be located with some degree of accuracy, providing care is used.

1. With wrist or pocket watch (Reference, page 8)

If your watch is running and set to standard time, hold it in your fingers or in your palm with the face parallel with the ground. Point the hour hand in the direction of the sun. Between six in the morning and six at night (6 A.M. to 6 P.M.), half the angle between the hour hand and the numeral twelve will be the general direction of true South. True North will, of course, be opposite. Take a number of readings and use the average.

Your watch may also be used on cloudy days by holding a small, straight twig in the center of the watch face and rotating the watch until the shadow created by the twig falls on the hour hand. South will be half the distance between the shadow and the numeral 12.

2. By shadow triangulation (Reference, page 9)

The method diagrammed on page 9 is a more accurate method for locating North. If your watch has stopped, you may estimate sun time fairly accurately by setting your watch to 12 noon when the center stake described in the diagram casts the shortest shadow.

3. Using the North Star

Travel at night especially through broken country is not recommended. The danger of falling into weed choked ravines, into bogs, and over fallen logs creates hazards which cannot be justified.

Limited travel may be attempted in bright moonlight in open country especially in arid regions in order to escape the heat of the day. Under such circumstances added vigilance must be used! Use the North Star as a guide if you must travel at night.

If you are not traveling at night, scribe the direction of the North Star in the ground or use sticks or stones to make a diagram. This will give you a guide when you start out in the morning.

4. Final suggestions

a. When you stop at any time during your trek, mark the direction you are traveling. Often times you may become confused in your directions after spending an hour or so resting or eating.

b. In the Northern Hemisphere at noon in the summer, the sun will be almost directly overhead. In the winter it will be due south of your position.

c. When traveling, pick out some guide point a good distance ahead. Continue to walk toward it. In the event that you should be forced to make a detour because of a swamp, etc., your guide point will put you back on the right course. When you reach your guide point, pick out another one farther ahead and so on.

FINDING DIRECTION BY WATCH

1. HOLD WATCH FLAT IN FINGERS OR IN PALM OF HAND.
2. ROTATE UNTIL THE HOUR HAND POINTS IN THE DIRECTION OF THE SUN.
3. BETWEEN 6AM AND 6 PM (STANDARD TIME), A LINE DIVIDING THE DISTANCE BETWEEN THE HOUR HAND AND THE NUMERAL 12 WILL POINT TRUE SOUTH.
4. DISREGARD THE MINUTE HAND.

IN THE GRAPHIC EXAMPLE, SOUTH IS THE LINE "A" AND IS EQUIDISTANT FROM THE HOUR OF 3 AND NUMERAL 12.

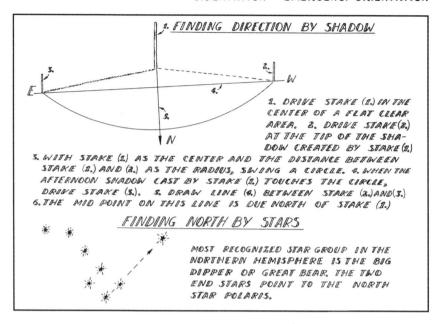

1. FINDING DIRECTION BY SHADOW

1. DRIVE STAKE (1.) IN THE CENTER OF A FLAT CLEAR AREA. 2. DRIVE STAKE(2.) AT THE TIP OF THE SHADOW CREATED BY STAKE (1.) 3. WITH STAKE (1.) AS THE CENTER AND THE DISTANCE BETWEEN STAKE (1.) AND (2.) AS THE RADIUS, SWING A CIRCLE. 4. WHEN THE AFTERNOON SHADOW CAST BY STAKE (1.) TOUCHES THE CIRCLE, DRIVE STAKE (3.). 5. DRAW LINE (4.) BETWEEN STAKE (2.) AND (3.) 6. THE MID POINT ON THIS LINE IS DUE NORTH OF STAKE (1.)

FINDING NORTH BY STARS

MOST RECOGNIZED STAR GROUP IN THE NORTHERN HEMISPHERE IS THE BIG DIPPER OR GREAT BEAR. THE TWO END STARS POINT TO THE NORTH STAR POLARIS.

THE PSYCHOLOGY OF BEING LOST & FOUND

Good mental attitude forms the foundation on which a successful survival experience is built.

It might be presumed that one possessing a good knowledge of woods lore would automatically be calm, cool, and collected in a survival situtation. Potentially, one possessing such knowledge is prepared for the challenge providing he is able to cope with the fear and frustrations encountered. Too often, however, he is not.

By comparison, lost children often react more logically — and with much less knowledge. Naturally there are cases of children fleeing in terror because of real or imaginary beasts giving chase. But they usually stay relatively near paths and when found are not too far from the point where they disappeared.

The child fails to recognize the potential seriousness of the situation. A good cry occasionally calms him down and as is so often the case, crying results in sleep. What could be better to relieve tension? It will also allow the searchers more time to find the child before he has the chance to wander too far.

An adult, on the other hand, recognizes the situation and as is so often the case, feels an overwhelming sense of urgency to find his way. He walks — or worse yet runs — aimlessly. If this occurs, he may end up 15 – 20 miles from his intended goal — in a highly confused mental state and physically exhausted.

9

This is a good example of the adult mind working more as a deterrent than as an aid. If he had used his superior powers of reason to control his fear and to allow him time to sit quietly and think things through, the situation would have been much less serious.

The importance of remaining calm, cool, and collected cannot be overstated! If panic remains primary, yell, throw rocks, cry, take a swim, take a nap, etc. No matter how compelled one feels to run, it is essential that he sit quietly, collect his thoughts, and generally review the situation.

He should take stock of the equipment he has and think of uses for each item. A mental picture of the general terrain may recall hills, streams, power lines, a specific dead tree, or a road.

Remaining quiet may also allow one to hear a distant train or auto horn. A commercial plane overhead can help in determining direction.

A survey of surroundings may indicate edible plants, animal paths leading to water, a good spot for a shelter, or a cleared site suitable for a signal fire.

These first few calm minutes can easily be the most important of the entire ordeal.

In most instances one's primary desire would be to travel. Psychologically, travel would mean going some place, hopefully that some place would be back to civilization. At the same time, however, careful consideration should be given to other aspects of the situation which might prove, in the final analysis, that travel would be a waste of time and energy — and a serious mistake.

A history of heart condition, diabetes, ambulatory impairment, bad eyesight, etc. should be carefully weighed before starting out. Swampy terrain, deep snow, extreme heat, etc. are conditions that should be carefully studied. Oftentimes a decision to stay put and signal for assistance may prove by far the best course of action.

Pride or embarrassment should not influence any decision one might make. Human life is infinitely more important!

Whatever one's decision might be — staying put or traveling — it is important that one establish certain routines and do certain morale lifting exercises. It is far better to look ahead toward specific tasks and hazards than to live only for the moment.

Food for thought as you contemplate being lost & found:

1. Restrict night travel. Deep shadows can hide natural hazards. Limited night travel may be attempted in open country, specifically in desert areas where extreme heat is a problem during the daylight hours.

2. Travel by water may prove easier by far than traveling the shore. Improvise a raft for equipment and clothing. Hold on to a log for added buoyancy and off you go! Be wary of rapids. If caught in one, keep your legs pointed downstream. They will act as spring boards in avoiding injury from rocks.

3. If traveling overland, remember that a straight line is the shortest distance between two points. Try to find a point of reference near you and one in the distance. Walk along the imaginary line between them. Repeat the process.

4. If you were lost during a hike or hunting trip, attempt to back track, imagining your current location as the hub of a wheel. Walk in complete circles around that hub, increasing the diameter each time until you can barely see your reference hub. Examine the ground for footprints, freshly broken sticks, trampled grass or weeds, etc. If successful, keep moving your reference hub and repeating the circular search pattern. This process has worked many times.

5. Use as much fresh water as possible, keeping in mind that in warm climates as much as a quart a day might not be sufficient.

6. In the absence of water or when water is scarce, suck pebbles.

7. Bathe often. If you are wearing socks, keep them dry and wash them frequently.

8. Keep your eyes constantly peeled for food. Eat at any time that food is available. This would be especially true if traveling. If staying put and maintaining a survival camp, it would probably prove advantageous to establish a schedule of everyday life and to stick to it as much as possible.

9. Regardless of your amount of food, eat minimum amounts of bitter varieties while consuming maximum amounts of bland or sweet varieties. If traveling in rough country, travel slowly and try to restrict your movements to a maximum of two miles per hour. Even in flat country your travel should be limited, restricting it to no more than 3½ miles per hour. At approximately the end of each hour, stop and rest for 10 to 15 minutes, being sure your legs are elevated.

10. If you possess fire building material and equipment, build a fire each night. Fire creates a degree of security.

11. Build a shelter each night — it too can boost one's morale.

12. Build signal fires as practical, keeping in mind that most forested areas are guarded by fire towers. Being careful not to start a forest fire, build a fire with caution and create as much smoke as you can. Although the fire guard may be at some distance, you will undoubtedly attract attention quickly.

13. Keep telling yourself, "I can do it."

WATER

(Charts, page 17)

Many persons have the mistaken idea that food is the most important item of survival. Unquestionably, food is an important item. Without water, however, food loses much of its importance in sustaining life.

An unequipped person may find it extremely difficult to obtain the quart of water that the body needs each day. Furthermore, his lack of knowledge about water that he may find could lead him into many pitfalls in regards to health. A few basic facts may be of assistance in obtaining the most desirable results.

1. Although extreme thirst may make a person desire large amounts of water, once a drinking source is obtained — BE CAUTIOUS! Rather than drinking large amounts of water in short periods, drink small quantities slowly over extended periods.

2. If you are overheated from strenuous exercise or from the heat of the day, avoid very cold water. It is also important at such times to refrain from consuming large amounts. Again, sip slowly over time.

3. During the winter months when eating snow or ice, do not swallow immediately. Hold the liquid in the mouth and allow it to warm since very cold water has a tendency to lower body temperature.

WATER & WELL-BEING

Prior to World War II several studies were undertaken to determine man's daily requirements of water under various survival conditions. As a rule of thmb, one pint per day was thought to be sufficient. The pint-per-day rule failed to consider the needs of a man in the shade versus one in the sun, the average mean temperature, food consumption, body exertion, body water balance at the beginning of the ordeal, etc.

However, by war's end, many tests had been made which when coupled with actual survival data covering a full range of conditions, gave considerably more accurate requirement data.

For example to maintain body water balance at a mean temperature of 90 degrees, a person must have more than 6 pints of water per day. At 50 degrees, the daily requirement drops to about 3 pints.

At the same time, life may be sustained for various lengths of time with less than the aforesaid amounts although body water balance will not be maintained, and slow dehydration and eventual death will occur.

At 120 degrees, a man in the shade, inactive, and with no calorie intake may survive for 2 days without any water but only for approximately 5 days with 20 quarts!

In a temperature of 90 degrees, he may sustain life for 7 days with no water and up to 23 days with 20 quarts.

Finally, at 50 degrees, he may survive for 10 days without water and up to a month with 20 quarts.

In climates of extreme high temperature, death usually occurs at about 15% dehydration. Regardless of climatic condition, 25% dehydration is probably fatal.

Signs of dehydration include laziness and lack of interest and initiative. Nausea usually occurs at about 5% dehydration with growing dizziness, severe headache, tingling in the limbs, difficulty in speech, and inability to walk. Delirium is common above 10% dehydration and the senses fail.

It seems unnecessary to again stress the importance of water in successfully pulling through a survival ordeal. If one recognizes daily requirements based on temperature and general conditions, he should accept the prime need to take whatever steps are necessary to obtain it in sufficient quantities to maintain health.

LOCATING WATER

If one learns some basic rules and terminology in regards to water, finding enough to sustain life will not be difficult.

The term "water table" may generally be defined as the surface below which water is pure. A water table usually follows the contour of the land above it, but may occasionally come to the surface to form seepage areas, springs, lakes, streams, swamps, etc.

Water occurring above the water table is defined as run-off water and is much more likely to be contaminated. Items to remember about water are listed here and are also shown graphically on page 19.

1. Water in the river must be regarded as unsafe for human consumption since it passes an area of heavy population.

2. Water in the lake is pure for drinking providing it is taken a good distance from the populated area.

3. Swamp water may be regarded as safe to drink if free from outside pollution from farming areas, seepage from town dumps, etc. I would suggest that this water be boiled to be safe.

4. Spring water is usually safe, especially if it is issuing from a rock formation.

5. Ground water will be very near the surface on a flood plain and is usually safe for drinking providing it is not too close to an inhabited area.

6. Desert water holes usually yield pure water provided that animals and birds drink from it. Keep a look-out for signs. If you are lost in a desert area, you may be directed to water by observing the flight of birds and following animals tracks.

7. Occasionally you may come upon areas in a desert region with lush foilage but with no signs of water. In such instances water is usually only a short distance below the surface and may usually be regarded as pure for drinking.

8. Snow and rain are pure.

9. Water in mountain streams is pure providing the streams have not passed inhabited areas.

14

Besides the more obvious ways of obtaining water, it is possible to locate plants which will yield quantities of water sufficient to sustain life. Grapevines yield an amazing quantity of water providing a prescribed procedure is followed in obtaining it. Cut the vine as high off the ground as possible and keep the cut end well elevated. Then cut off the lower end and let the water drip into your mouth or into a container. When the sap ceases to flow, cut a few more inches from the elevated end and the water will flow again. Repeat the process until the vine is dry.

Probably most of you are aware of the barrel cactus as a ready source of water in desert regions. Having had experience obtaining water in this fashion while on archaeological trips in Arizona, I found the water somewhat unpleasant but not unpalatable. Remove the top of the cactus and crush the pulpy center with a stick using a downward and outward motion. Water will fill the cavity. It is also possible to cut pulpy sections to chew or to save for future use.

The dew from tree and bush leaves is also pure, and with a little patience, considerable water may be collected in the manner. As an experiment, I collected dew by patting leaves with a cotton cloth and then wringing the water into a cup. In 20 minutes, I had collected a cupful.

COLLECTING WATER
(Diagram, page 16)

An advanced method of obtaining drinking water has developed because of the availability of plastic sheeting. If one possesses a piece, it is possible to obtain some water even in an arid region.

The system works as follows: Dig or scrape out a hole in the ground to a depth determined by the moisture content of the soil. In relatively moist soil, a hole 12" in depth may prove to be sufficient, while in a desert area one may have to go to a depth of 3 feet or more. The hole should be dug in an open area free of shade. The size of the hole will depend on the size of the plastic sheeting one possesses. At the bottom and in the center of the hole, place a container capable of holding water.

Lay the plastic over the top of the hole and weight it down with rocks around the edges. When this operation is completed, the sheeting should be relatively loose. Make certain at the same time that the edges of the sheeting are tight against the ground surface so that air circulation into the pit is eliminated.

In the center of the sheeting directly above the water container that you placed in the bottom of the pit, place a stone, not heavy enough to break through the plastic, but heavy enough to depress the center to form a large cone.

In principle, moisture will be drawn from the soil and will condense into water droplets on the underside of the plastic sheet. As these droplets combine into larger drops they will run down to the lowest point on the

15

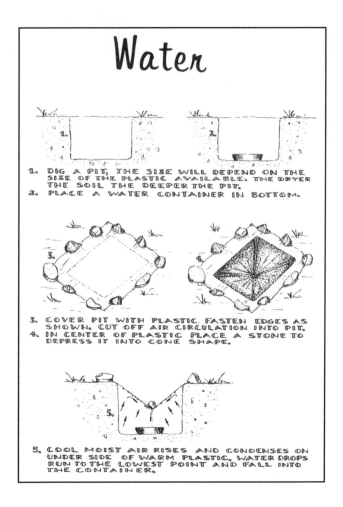

Water

1. DIG A PIT, THE SIZE WILL DEPEND ON THE SIZE OF THE PLASTIC AVAILABLE. THE DRYER THE SOIL THE DEEPER THE PIT.
2. PLACE A WATER CONTAINER IN BOTTOM.

3. COVER PIT WITH PLASTIC. FASTEN EDGES AS SHOWN. CUT OFF AIR CIRCULATION INTO PIT.
4. IN CENTER OF PLASTIC PLACE A STONE TO DEPRESS IT INTO CONE SHAPE.

5. COOL MOIST AIR RISES AND CONDENSES ON UNDER SIDE OF WARM PLASTIC. WATER DROPS RUN TO THE LOWEST POINT AND FALL INTO THE CONTAINER.

plastic (below the stone) and drop off into the water container below.

The amounts of water obtainable in this manner will be dependent upon the percentage of moisture in the soil in relationship to the surface temperature of the sheeting. This in turn is dependent upon the heat of the sun and/or temperature.

It is doubtful that one may obtain ample water by this method to satisfy body requirements, especially in a desert area. The method will also require considerable time. However, knowing the importance of water, one should not be hasty in discarding the method or abandoning the process once undertaken unless absolutely necessary.

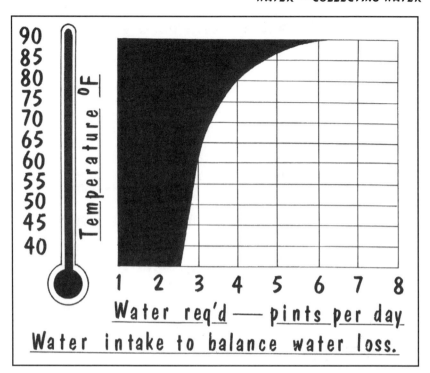

Water intake to balance water loss.

Temperature in the shade	EXPECTED DAYS OF SURVIVAL					
120°	2	2	2	2 plus	3	4 plus
110°	3	3	3 plus	4	5	7
100°	5	5 plus	6	7	9 plus	13 plus
90°	7	8	9	10 plus	15	23
80°	9	10	11	13	19	29
70°	10	11	12	14	20 plus	32
60°	10	11	12	14	21	32
50°	10	11	12	14 plus	21	32
Amounts of water available	None	1 qt.	2 qt.	4 qt.	10 qt.	20 qt.

CLEANING & CLEARING WATER

There are a number of different methods for cleaning and clearing water *before purification.*

Although the procedure is not absolutely necessary, the psychological advantages to the user make the procedure worthwhile.

Pouring water through several layers of tight mesh cloth will remove some matter from the water and is the quickest method but not the most thorough. A bark funnel with a sand-filled cloth in the small end will also remove sediment.

If you are near a muddy pool or swamp, dig a small well a few feet from it and allow the water to seep in. Bail out the first muddy flow and then allow the water to clear itself.

The root of the opuntia or prickly pear cactus may also be used for clearing water. Its gelatinous tissue will collect sediment.

WATER PURIFICATION
(Chart, page 19)

In North America, serious health hazards, dysentery, cholera, and typhoid being the most common, may result from drinking impure water. Consequently, any water which you are not certain is safe for drinking should be purified before it is used for drinking and before it is used to wash foods that are to be eaten raw.

Boiling water vigorously is the most foolproof method of disinfecting. Water should be placed in a clean container and boiled for at least five minutes. Because boiling removes air from the water and makes it taste flat, the condition can be remedied by pouring water back and forth between clean containers or stirring vigorously to aerate the pure water.

Chemical disinfectants should be regarded only as emergency methods in disinfecting water.

1. **Halazone Tablets.** Use two tablets per quart of water. Allow it to stand for ½ hour. It should have a chlorine smell. If it does not, it will need further purification before using. Add additional tablets one at a time.

2. **Laundry bleach** also works well in the ration of 10 drops to 1 gallon of water. As with halazone tablets, add an additional drop if water has no chlorine smell. A small plastic container of chlorine bleach can be easily carried with you while in the wilderness.

3. **Iodine** may also be used in water disinfecting in the ratio of 1 drop per quart of water. Caution in using this method is suggested for those with glandular trouble.

If your supply of water seems to have a strong unpleasant odor, take a small amount of fresh charcoal from the fire, add it to the water, and boil. Charcoal will remove most of the unpleasant odor.

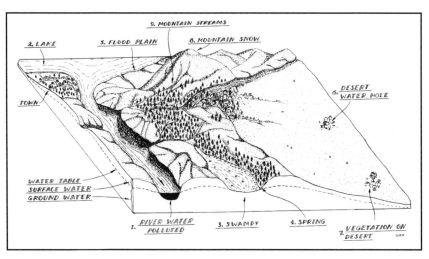

9. MOUNTAIN STREAMS
8. MOUNTAIN SNOW
2. LAKE
5. FLOOD PLAIN
DESERT
6. WATER HOLE
TOWN
WATER TABLE
SURFACE WATER
GROUND WATER
RIVER WATER
1. POLLUTED
3. SWAMPY
4. SPRING
VEGETATION ON
7. DESERT

BARREL CACTUS
SOURCE OF PURE
DESERT WATER

OPUNTIA
(PRICKLY PEAR CACTUS)
TO CLEAR WATER

NEVER SHORT-CUT WATER PURIFICATION!

BOIL 3-5
MINUTES   OR   ADD HALAZONE
2 TABS PER QT.   OR   2-3 DROPS
IODINE

CHARCOAL ADDED TO WATER
AND BOILED VIGOROUSLY WILL
REMOVE UNPLEASANT ODOR.

REMEMBER!
1. USE OPUNTIA CACTUS TO CLEAR WATER.
2. USE CHARCOAL TO REMOVE ODOR.
3. PURIFY BY BOILING, ADDING HALAZONE
   OR IODINE.
4. NEVER ASSUME CLEAR AND ODOR
   FREE WATER IS PURE!

AVOID DYSENTERY & TYPHOID.

19

SHELTERS & BEDS

SHELTERS
(Diagrams, pages 21 & 22)

Shelters and beds must be discussed together since, in most instances, the absence of one minimizes the effectiveness of the other. A warm snug shelter and a comfortable bed will go far to boost morale.

Most everyone who has ever done any wilderness camping will agree that a camp is really not a camp until the tent is up, bed roll laid out, and a fire built. In establishing a survival camp there are a number of things to consider.

1. Will it be for overnight or for a few days? A camp set up for several days may afford you the opportunity to get organized.
2. Are there building materials nearby?
3. Is there good water available?
4. Is there wild food and game in the area?
5. Are there many mosquitoes or crawling bugs that may cause discomfort?
6. Is there a good fuel supply?
7. Is there protection against the weather if it is needed?
8. Is the camp situated in a safe location? Stay clear of areas near rock falls, haunts of predatory animals, and dry stream beds that may come roaring to life without warning.

Once a good site has been selected, a shelter may be built with the materials available. No matter what type of shelter you decide to build, it will be worthwhile to do a good job.

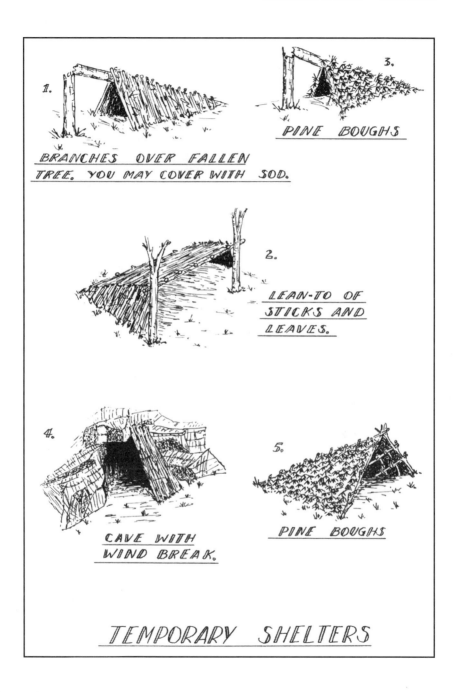

1.

BRANCHES OVER FALLEN
TREE. YOU MAY COVER WITH SOD.

3.

PINE BOUGHS

2.

LEAN-TO OF
STICKS AND
LEAVES.

4.

CAVE WITH
WIND BREAK.

5.

PINE BOUGHS

TEMPORARY SHELTERS

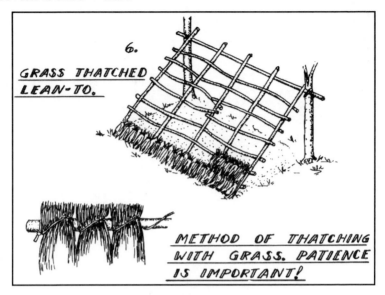

6.

GRASS THATCHED LEAN-TO.

METHOD OF THATCHING WITH GRASS. PATIENCE IS IMPORTANT!

BEDS
(Diagrams, page 23)

A good night's sleep will do wonders for a person. Under survival conditions, it cannot be over-emphasized! Sleep will give you renewed vigor and and improved outlook on your situation. Exhaustion will destroy morale and sap body strength.

Once your campsite has been located, a good bed should not be hard to construct. Follow a few simple rules and you should have few problems.

1. Build your bed on a slight slope with your head elevated.
2. Select an area free of rocks.
3. Build your bed of dry material; do not use green foliage.
4. Follow other rules as outlined in finding a good campsite.

Ground beds are suggested as the best under most conditions. There may be isolated instances where an elevated bed may prove more satisfactory, such as when nothing but mud or swampy land is available or when there may be a serious problem with crawling insects. Ground beds fall into three categories: 1. Log and leaf bed; 2. Pine bough bed; 3. Grass mat bed. Figure 1 and 2 on page 23 show construction methods for all three types.

There are a few hints relative to ground beds which may also be useful. In cold or extremely damp weather, build a fire over the area where you intend making your bed. Keep the fire going for 2 – 3 hours and then rake it away and make your bed. It will be very helpful in giving your bed warmth and will also help in eliminating moisture from your building material.

Remember that in order to stay warm, it is more necessary to insulate from the ground below than from the air above.

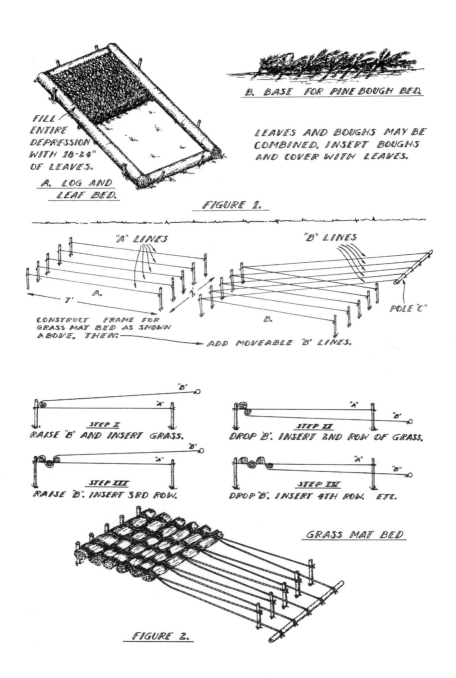

FILL ENTIRE DEPRESSION WITH 18-24" OF LEAVES.

A. LOG AND LEAF BED.

B. BASE FOR PINE BOUGH BED.

LEAVES AND BOUGHS MAY BE COMBINED. INSERT BOUGHS AND COVER WITH LEAVES.

FIGURE 1.

"A" LINES

"B" LINES

7'

A.

B.

POLE "C"

CONSTRUCT FRAME FOR GRASS MAT BED AS SHOWN ABOVE. THEN:—

ADD MOVEABLE "B" LINES.

STEP I
RAISE "B" AND INSERT GRASS.

STEP II
DROP "B". INSERT 2ND ROW OF GRASS.

STEP III
RAISE "B". INSERT 3RD ROW.

STEP IV
DROP "B". INSERT 4TH ROW. ETC.

GRASS MAT BED

FIGURE 2.

YOUR KNIFE
(Diagrams, pages 25 & 26)

In 1938, I was presented my first and only sheath knife. Although the blade is now a little shorter and not quite as broad as it was, it is still an item of prime importance on all fishing, hunting, and hiking expeditions.

Treat a good knife like an old friend. Don't abuse it! Keep it sharp, clean, and well-protected. It should not be used for mumbly-peg, knife throwing, stirring fires, roasting marshmallows or opening cans. A good knife will prove to be an invaluable asset if all of your other equipment were lost, and it will afford you greater survival opportunities and an added degree of security.

Throughout the years, I have seen many instances of knives being improperly used and nearly as many instances of loss and breakage due to improper sheathing.

The conventional sheath knife, the A knife on page 25, is secured in the sheath by a snapped loop which closes around the handle. The sheath is fastened to the belt through slits in the sheath under the knife handle. It is a common occurrence to have the snap on the blade handle open accidentally by catching on a branch or by rubbing the coat sleeve against it. The snap may also be forced open if the knife is worn too far around on the small of the back. When sitting down, the pressure of the blade against your body may force out on the handle and disengage the snap. Worse yet, you may break off the blade.

Knife B shows the type of sheath I prefer. It requires no snap on the handle and eliminates most of the chance of loss or breaking the blade and still holds the knife securely in place.

Some feel that a sheath knife should be worn in such a manner that it can be grasped very quickly: "The fastest knife in the woods." Since we aren't playing "good guys versus bad guys," let's not worry about that phase of things!

The type of sheath I suggest is certainly not new — having been used long before the modern snap was invented. By extending the full sheath about ¾ of the way up the handle, the need for a snap is eliminated. Instead, the sheath is secured to the belt with two leather thongs. I feel that this system of sheathing minimizes the chances of loss, eliminates the cause of breaking the blade, and still allows the knife to be grasped easily.

Knife C is nothing more than a conventional waterproof match case. I always carry one fastened to the bottom of my knife sheath. Since my sheath is never removed from my belt and in event that I should lose all my other gear through some mishap, I know that I will still be in possession of two very important survival items — a good, sharp knife and a supply of matches.

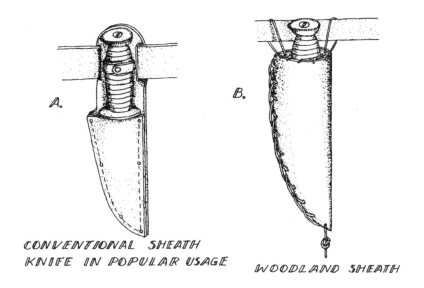

A.

CONVENTIONAL SHEATH
KNIFE IN POPULAR USAGE

B.

WOODLAND SHEATH

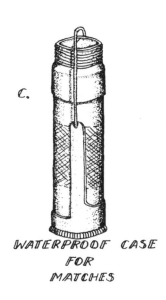

C.

WATERPROOF CASE
FOR
MATCHES

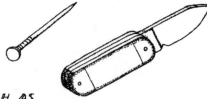

1. SELECT STONE SUCH AS FLINT, PYRITE, QUARTZ, QUARTZITE OR OTHER VERY HARD VARIETIES.
2. STEEL FROM MISCELLANEOUS SOURCES MAY BE USED.
3. STRIKE EDGE OF STONE WITH STEEL.
4. DIRECT SPARKS INTO THE TINDER.
5. TINDER MAY BE CHARRED CLOTH, DRY MOSS, PUNK, DOWN, DRY FUNGI, ETC.

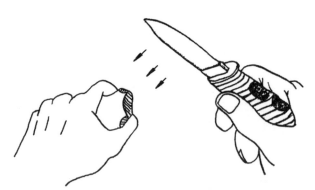

GRASP THE FLINT AND STEEL AS SHOWN THEN STRIKE EDGE OF FLINT. PRACTICE WILL TEACH YOU HOW TO DIRECT SPARK.

FLINT & STEEL

LEATHER CORD VS. KNIFE

If you found yourself lost or stranded in a wilderness area wearing only a bathing suit and had a choice of a single piece of survival equipment — a knife or a leather cord — which would you choose?

Unless one found himself in such a position and was forced to make such a choice, the question would remain purely academic. However, the idea has been the center of many lively discussions and as would be expected, the results — inconclusive.

You have probably made your choice and more than likely selected the knife. Among its potential uses you probably included a few of those listed below.

1. Protection
2. Hunting animals for food
3. Aid in constructing shelters
4. Aid in gathering bark for utensils
5. Aid in gathering materials for medicines
6. Making a bow
7. Gathering bark to make rope and fish line, etc.
8. Making fish hooks
9. Making a spear
10. Etc.
11. Etc.

The list is rather extensive and would suggest that the knife is without peer, especially if compared with a relatively limited list of uses for the cord.

1. Firebow string for making fire by friction
2. Bow string for bow and arrow (protection and food)
3. Noose for snare
4. Fish line
5. Etc.
6. Etc.

The following pages will review the value of the knife and cord as survival equipment. The potential uses of each will be discussed and whenever and wherever possible, alternates for each will be suggested. Hopefully when completed, we will be in a better position to select that item which most closely matches the overall requirements for the best single piece of survival equipment. But the final test rests with the person who is lost. His ability will ultimately offer the proof.

Water, food, and fire should be one's primary concerns. If one can find water, secure ample food, and be successful in making fire, the three primary survival necessities have been obtained.

FIRE PRODUCTION

Presuming that one finds water by some means, fire should then become the primary goal. Fire should be regarded as the heart of one's existence around which revolves all other phases of the endeavor. Fire affords heat for cooking and warmth, light, protection, security, and a method of signaling for help.

How does one make fire? With a knife available, the flint and steel method would be the natural choice. No finer and faster makeshift method for producing fire is possible than striking flint with steel, providing that the conditions are right and proper combustible material is available or accessible.

In principle, fire by flint and steel is produced by creating sparks which fall into an easily ignited tinder. Charred cloth is by far the most acceptable tinder and most inaccessible under survival conditions. Flint or other spark-producing stones may also prove to be difficult to obtain. Dampness, rain, and wind can make this method of fire starting impossible.

Producing fire by friction, on the other hand, is much less affected by climatic conditions and/or wind since the friction method creates small glowing particles rather than sparks like the striking method. These glowing particles last longer than flint sparks and require a somewhat less inflammable and much more easily obtainable tinder. Shredded cedar bark, for example, works well.

The fire bow string is the essential item in fire by friction equipment, except in the case of the fire trough. It is questionable that any type of wilderness material can be used to construct a cord strong enough to withstand the stress exerted with a fire bow string.

It would therefore seem that a leather cord affords the best possible advantages in creating fire in the greatest variety of circumstances.

WEAPONRY, FOOD PROCUREMENT & SHELTER CONSTRUCTION
(Diagram, page 31)

We have all read spine chilling reports of successful hand-to-hand combat with bears, wolves, and mountain lions, using only a knife. Most such stories were true. However, in most of these incidents the winner was severely mauled or permanently disabled or disfigured.

It is therefore doubtful that a hand-held knife should be regarded as the best protective weapon against such adversaries.

Most obviously the knife could be fastened to a long pole to fashion a spear. Better yet, a spear or spears could be fashioned by sharpening the poles to a point with the knife.

A spear equally as good or better can be fashioned by placing the end of a pole in a fire. By carefully controlling the burning, it is possible to fashion a point by rubbing away the charred portion. The point will be sharp and the heat will also tend to harden it.

During a *Michigan Outdoors* rally I was fortunate in having the opportunity to discuss the construction and handling of a spear with Mr. Les Perrine of Houghton Lake, Michigan.

Mr. Perrine is a dedicated woodsman who spends much of his time in the Canadian wilderness. Since the Canadian government restricts the use of firearms even for protection, Mr. Perrine was forced to adopt and use the spear for protection and so far has successfully killed many bears in combat.

The spear is not thrown or jabbed. Rather the blunt end is held at ground level and underfoot. By holding the angularly elevated shaft with both arms and moving forward or backward around the pivot point, it is possible to follow the stalking animal and keep the pointed end directed at the attacker. If one is actually attacked, the blunt end of the spear will hold and the weight of the attacker will force it on to the spear.

A short cross arm is also mounted on the spear shaft about 18" from the pointed end. This addition will stop the body from being completely impaled and injuring you as it falls.

A spear could also prove valuable in spearing fish and killing slow moving animals such as the porcupine. Whatever the case, a wooden spear fashioned without a knife could do as acceptable a job as a whittled one.

The knife would also prove valuable in constructing various types of traps and snares although a leather cord would prove nearly indispensable for the actual noose. Again I question whether any wilderness materials would work as well in constructing a noose unless the user was a veteran woodsman.

Neither the knife nor the leather cord would be essential in constructing shelters. Wilderness areas are amply supplied with material requiring only a little know-how and patience to construct shelters of a very useable type.

A knife would be helpful in collecting materials to make utensils and fish hooks, collecting wild edible plants, bark for medicinal purposes, arrows, bows, etc.

However, the value of a cord in making fire and the value of fire in other survival activities would, I feel, continue to overshadow the absolute necessity of selecting the knife as the one basic piece of original equipment.

In the first edition of this book, I discussed in some detail the construction of some tools. As you read the materials in a later chapter on stone tools, note that excellent stone tools can be constructed with patience and practice. Useful arrow points and very useable knife blades can be made. The knife especially will make a very useable substitute for the steel one.

A bow and arrows might prove useful additions to your equipment. Again as in the case of the fire bow, it is questionable that any survival materials could be used to make a bow string strong enough to withstand the strain placed upon it. Again we rely on the leather cord and use whatever improvised equipment — and stone tools to fashion the bow and arrows. Difficult, yes! But impossible? No!

Certainly the production of survival tying material would not be dependent upon the knife. Outer bark — useless as cordage — could be removed by striking the tree surface with a stone or club in order to expose the useable material. Once exposed a sharp-edged stone could be used to cut it free at the end after which the fibers could be pulled loose in long strips and woven together.

Would you still select the knife or does the cord now seem to be the best possible selection?

We have pretty well covered both the uses of the knife and the leather cord and have shown where the cord can be substituted for the knife or where the cord is more important and also where both tools could be eliminated. You probably have additional thoughts on one or more of the points discussed. Good! The deeper one is willing to dig into a subject the more is discovered — and the more is learned about it.

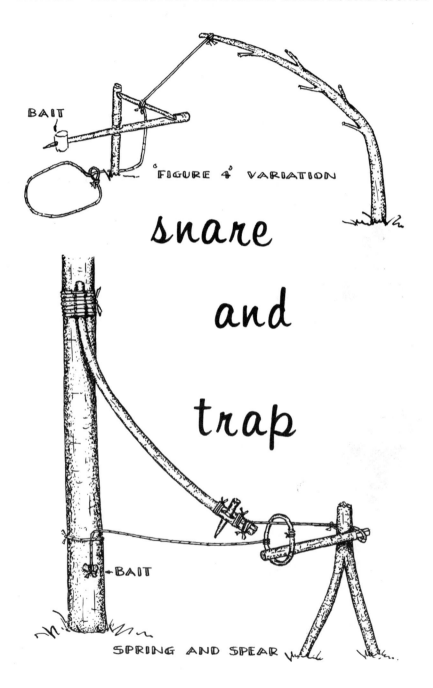

BAIT

'FIGURE 4' VARIATION

snare

and

trap

BAIT

SPRING AND SPEAR

31

FIRE

Under survival conditions, a fire can prove to be one of your greatest assets. Undoubtedly, there have been a number of instances while on camping, hunting, or fishing trips that a cheery warm fire would have been a welcome addition — and was!

If one is lost or stranded in a wilderness area, the importance of fire is multiplied many times. It will afford warmth, an aid in food preparation, a rescue signal, and above all, will add a sense of security to an otherwise bleak situation.

TECHNIQUES FOR FIRE STARTING

At best a fire is difficult to make without matches. A good magnifying lens will provide one method if the sun is shining. A suitable lens may be secured from a pair of binoculars, a camera or in certain instances, from a flashlight or wrist watch.

Flint and steel seems the most well-known method for starting a fire. Quartz, flint, or other types of hard stone struck with a piece of metal such as a nail, knife, watchcase or belt buckle will create sparks. With the proper tinder and a little practice directing sparks into the tinder, a fire can be kindled rapidly in this manner. The diagram on page 26 gives illustrations and instructions for this method of fire starting.

Making fire by friction involves several different techniques. A survey of methods from various parts of the world indicates that in the hands of experts, the friction method may be almost as fast as striking a match. I have included only two methods. I cannot judge the reliability of either as compared to other friction methods.

BOW AND DRILL METHOD

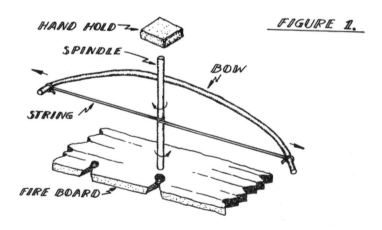

The bow and drill method shown is the most common friction system. The fire board and spindle should be made from a piece of dry and well-seasoned soft wood such as willow or cottonwood. If you are near a cut bank stream, look for exposed roots — and be sure they are dry since they are ideal. The fire board need not be large. A 2-inch-wide piece that is 5 or 6 inches long should do the trick. Make the spindle at least 12 inches long as it will wear away rapidly. The hand hold should be made of some hard wood; a pine knot will work well. Cut a small depression in the underside to hold the spindle in position. A piece of softer wood with a small coin recessed slightly in the depression on the wood piece's underside will also work. Tallow may also be used to cut friction between the hand hold and the spindle to a minimum.

The bow should be approximately 24 inches long and made of some stiff springy wood that will keep the bow string taut. A shoe lace or a piece of rope will work for the bow string, although a leather cord is by far the best. To operate, kneel, placing the left knee on the edge of the fire board to steady it. Twist the bow string around the spindle, placing the lower end in the fire board depression. Grasp the hand hold in the left hand and steady the top end of the spindle. Operate the bow in a back and forth motion. The friction caused by the revolving spindle against the fire board will create fine carbon dust. The sparks will drop into the V cut in the fire board and into the tinder placed directly below it. As soon as sparks are discernable in the tinder, pick up the smoldering tinder in your cupped hands and gently blow the sparks to life. When a flame appears, quickly kindle your fire around it.

FIRE SAW METHOD

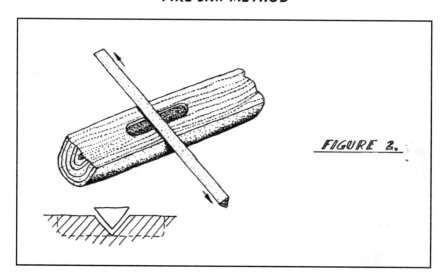

FIGURE 2.

The second friction method is commonly called a fire saw. Soft woods are used in construction. Sparks will build up in the depression shown, and the resulting sparks are carefully dropped into tinder and blown to life. This system requires hard work and is not the most successful although some practice may reward you with success.

KINDLING THE SPARK

There are a great many tinders that may be utilized and some are better than others. The inner bark of a long-dead, slippery or red elm makes excellent tinder. Dry seed down, moss, flower down, dry rotted wood, and pulverized plant fiber such as nettle are also worthy of consideration. However, charred cloth is by far the best tinder but obviously cannot be obtained until you have somehow managed to kindle a fire. Once obtained it should make future fire building much easier.

If one is fortunate enough to have a small metal container, a band aid box for example, the problem is solved. Fill the box with cloth, close the lid and place it in the fire. After a few minutes (trial and error), rake out the box and let it cool. Your tinder will be ready to use. Store any unused tinder in the container for future use.

If no metal container is available, roll ½" balls of cloth in clay. Puncture with two or three small holes. Allow these balls to dry by placing them near the fire for a day or longer if you can afford the time. When dry they can be placed in the fire. As before, the time necessary to properly char the cloth will be on a trial and error basis. Crack open the balls as necessary.

As a final suggestion, punk or dry, rotted wood will burn for many hours with a light red glow and no flame. Large chunks of this wood are obtainable in most wooded areas. Look for dead trees. Fire can be transported long distances by wedging burning punk in the split end of a green branch. Carry extra supplies of punk if available.

Never attempt to kindle a fire until all of the proper supplies have been collected. Having a supply of tinder is only the beginning. The sparks falling into the tinder must have fuel to ignite, shredded inner bark or dry grass for example. Blow softly! Once a flame has appeared, carefully add very small twigs or wood shavings and then slowly increase the size of the fuel as the fire gains strength. Lay out 4 or 5 graduated piles of fuel. The piles should range in size from the smallest twigs to branches 3" – 4" in diameter. Don't be hasty! Adding too much fuel too fast may snuff out the flame before it has a chance to grow strong.

WHERE TO BUILD THE FIRE

IF SOIL IS MOIST BUILD A PLATFORM OF LOGS OR STONE.

A STONE OR WOOD WIND BREAK WILL MAKE GOOD REFLECTORS TOO.

IF NO MATERIAL AVAILABLE, DIG A WIND PIT.

DON'T BUILD A FIRE UNDER A SNOW COVERED PINE TREE SINCE WIND OR HEAT MAY CAUSE SNOW TO FALL AND PUT OUT THE FIRE.

MAKE A WIND BREAK FROM BOUGHS.

FIRE BUILDING

Have you ever attempted to kindle a fire during a day outing or overnight when the temperature was below zero? You may have noted that the procedure seemed more difficult than during a summer outing. You may have known why or passed off the problem to damp wood. The problem may have been partly due to some moisture in the wood but was primarily due to the added heat needed to ignite the wood. The kindling point of wood is somewhere between 800° – 900°.

Assuming that we were going to build a summer campfire during an 80° day, we would be required to raise the wood to around 720° to reach the kindling point. Conversely, if we attempt to build a campfire at 30° below zero, we would need to raise the temperature of the wood an additional 110° or so, or a total of 830°, above the air temperature. In preparing a winter fire, much larger quantities of starter fuel such as shavings and small twigs will be needed since they build heat and ignite much faster than large sticks.

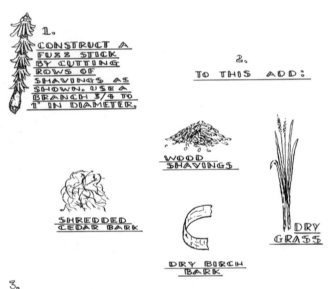

1. CONSTRUCT A FUZZ STICK BY CUTTING ROWS OF SHAVINGS AS SHOWN. USE A BRANCH 3/4 TO 1" IN DIAMETER.

2. TO THIS ADD:

WOOD SHAVINGS

SHREDDED CEDAR BARK

DRY BIRCH BARK

DRY GRASS

3. NEXT COLLECT AND STACK 3 PILES OF WOOD IN THE APPROXIMATE SIZES AS INDICATED.

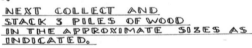

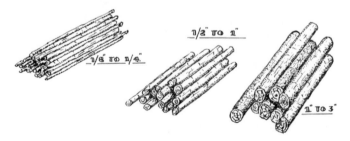

1/8" TO 1/4"

1/2" TO 1"

1" TO 3"

LAY THE FIRE BY PLACING THE FUZZ STICK
AS SHOWN.

OVER THE TOP ADD OTHER
EASILY COMBUSTIBLE MATERIALS.

CERTAIN TO LEAVE AN OPENING SO BE
MATCH CAN BE INSERTED. CONTINUE
AS SHOWN.

fire starters

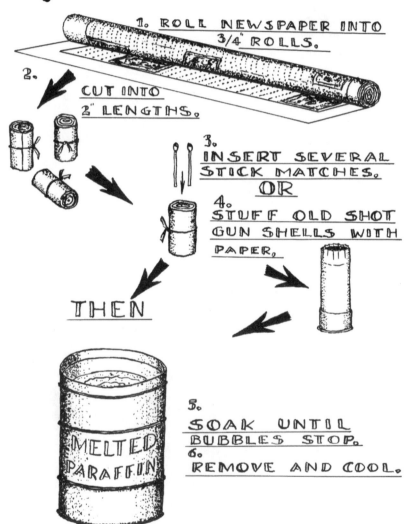

1. ROLL NEWSPAPER INTO 3/4" ROLLS.

2. CUT INTO 2" LENGTHS.

3. INSERT SEVERAL STICK MATCHES.

OR

4. STUFF OLD SHOT GUN SHELLS WITH PAPER,

THEN

MELTED PARAFFIN

5. SOAK UNTIL BUBBLES STOP.
6. REMOVE AND COOL.

FIRE STARTERS
(Diagram, page 38)

Once the fire is built and is burning well, collect a good quantity of fuel and stack it near the fire, both to dry and warm it for later use. On the basis of my own experiences, one might consider carrying a block of paraffin or a candle. A few chips of wax can be a great help in getting your fire underway. Fire starters can also be made by dipping 3 – 4 inch sections of tightly rolled newspaper in paraffin. Similar starters can also be made by stuffing used cardboard shotgun shells with sawdust and then dipping in paraffin. Either kind of fire starter can be further enhanced by including two or three stick matches before dipping. Carrying a starter or two can prove to be well worth the effort!

AN OUNCE OF PREVENTION

Learning to build a fire under various adverse conditions should be part of any survival training program. Failures in fire building occur often, not from lack of ability but because the procedures required for success are only partially followed or ignored.

If one has a supply of matches, a fire starter or lighter, it is still important to proceed with care to conserve them for use another day.

Regardless of the amount of rain, wind, snow or sub-zero temperature, it is quite possible to kindle a healthy fire and to keep it burning, providing that care is used in preparation, starting, and maintenance. The drawings accompanying this chapter present the basics. Practice makes perfect or nearly so! Improvise as needed.

SURVIVOR-FRIENDLY PLANTS

Anyone interested in the out-of-doors should have at least a passing acquaintance with the subject of wild plants. There are hundreds of edible varieties in North America. However, there are also many species ranging from mildly to deadly poisonous. Although there is not an abundance of books on the subject, those that are available are for the most part excellent.

Few areas are completely void of some edible variety. However, most persons are reluctant to try them especially since they fall into the general category of weeds. Furthermore, the word "edible" guarantees neither succulence nor palatability.

Regardless of the lack of guarantees, keep in mind that edible weeds offer varying amounts of nutritional value and are therefore important.

As a rule of thumb, if you are in doubt about any species, pass it by! Don't risk illness if it can be avoided. If you feel compelled to experiment, the following rules are suggested.

1. Rub a small amount of the plant juice from leaves and roots on the back of your hands and allow it to remain for a half-hour or so.
2. If there is no rash or redness, chew a small quantity and spit it out. *Swallow none of it.*
3. If no ill effects occur, chew and swallow a very small portion. Allow 4 – 6 hours for results.
4. If you still feel no ill effects, repeat the process several more times.
5. If you are still on your feet and well, it may be presumed that the plant is edible.
6. If there are any indications of poisoning, induce vomiting.

As a suggestion, the 12 – 18 hours spent in testing questionable foods might be better spent searching for known edible varieties.

Since it is unlikely that you will remain in one place during your wilderness ordeal, some thought should be given to collecting food for future use. This would be especially true if food availability is uncertain. Under such conditions, consider spending a day or two collecting supplies.

Bulbous roots, tubers, nuts, and leaves can be transported easily and will remain useable for long periods. Fruits and berries may also be kept for limited periods if transported in crushproof containers. Hard green fruit may also be carried and eaten as it ripens.

The following pages list and describe 42 varieties of edible wild herbaceous plants and 10 varieties of food trees, and 6 varieties of edible fungi in a following chapter. A few of the more common poisonous plants and fungi are also shown. For more complete information, consult your library. Good hunting!

In closing, I ask one favor. Many wild plants are becoming scarce. A few are almost non-existent. Familiarize yourself with the edible varieties — in the field, if possible, but do not destroy them. Be conservation conscious.

HERBACEOUS PLANTS
(Plates 1-14)

1. **ADDERSTONGUE** — Low plant 5" – 10" high consisting of a pair of mottled, oblong-elliptical leaves with a 6-petaled yellow, violet or white flower on a separate short stalk. *Plate 1*
Found: Moist woods, Early spring to late fall.
Food: Bulb is edible when cooked but eat sparingly. Young spring leaves sometimes used as greens.

2. **ARROWHEAD** — A small plant found in wet ground and shallow water. Arrow-shaped leaves appear at the end of individual stems. Flower appears on separate stem. *Plate 1*
Found: Wet ground and shallow water.
Food: Boiled or baked bulbs taste like potatoes. Follow the threadlike root to find the bulb.

3. **BRAKEN FERN (Brake or Fern Fiddleheads)** — A large fern showing dark green leaves on the upper side and lighter green on the under side. *Plate 1*
Found: Common in most of U.S., but prefers damp shade.
Food: Pick fiddleheads, remove fuzz, and boil until tender — very little food value. Grind rootstock and make into bread.

4. **BULRUSH** — A tall marsh, grass-like plant consisting of a long stem with small seeds at upper end. Light green in color. *Plate 2*
Found: Slow streams, marshes, edge of lakes.
Food: Base of stalk and young shoots are edible either raw or cooked. Young roots are also edible. Roots may be dried and pounded into flour.

5. **BURDOCK** — Large plant which may grow to height of 9 feet but averages somewhat less. Coarse leaves. Purplish florets compressed in burr-like heads. *Plate 2*
Found: Open wastelands, roadsides, along streams.
Food: Tender stalks may be peeled and eaten raw or cooked. Root may also be cleaned and cooked. Use two changes of water in all cooking.

6. **CATTAIL** — Tall stalks with flat leaves. Average height about 4 feet but may reach 6 feet. Flowers appear at top of stalk. *Plate 2*
Found: Wet and swampy areas year-round. Leaves die down in winter, but flower spike remains.
Food: Roots may be roasted or boiled, then chew out the starch. Young shoots may also be eaten. Root may also be dried and pounded into meal or cooked to form a thick soup. Young spikes before they flower are edible raw or cooked.

7. CHICORY — Light-blue flowers grow close along stiff branching stems averaging 3 feet in height. Flowers wither rapidly in sun.
Found: Pastures, roadsides, and waste places.
Food: Dried roots make good coffee substitute. Young spring leaves boiled in several changes of water resemble spinach. *Plate 3*

8. CLOVER — The blossoms, stems, and seeds are edible. Clean and dip in salt water, if possible. *Plate 3*

9. CRINKLEROOT OR TOOTHWART — Plants 8" – 15" tall with erect stems usually bearing two leaves as well as some that spring directly from the roots. Leaves stalked, each of three ovate-toothed leaflets. White flowers are in bunches on top of stem. *Plate 3*
Found: Eastern U.S. in deciduous forests.
Food: Crisp rootstock eaten raw or can be used as a salad ingredient. Resembles horseradish in flavor.

10. DANDELION — Well-known to all! *Plate 4*
Found: World wide.
Food: Roots may be eaten raw. Cook leaves as you would spinach. The vitamin A content of the dandelion is superior to most domesticated vegetables. Make tea by boiling the leaves, a good cold remedy.

11. FIREWEED — A tall plant which thrives in burned-over areas, growing to a height of from 2 to 5 or 6 feet. It has purple and pink flowers. *Plate 4*
Found: Burned-over areas, dry coal in fields, open woodlands, and along roads.
Food: Young shoots and leaves good raw or cooked. Add salt if possible.

12. CURLY DOCK — Tall plants growing from 25" – 40", deep tap roots, smooth many-margined leaves, long stems of small, greenish flowers fading to reddish-brown. *Plate 4*
Found: Waste places, pasture areas or in cultivated ground in temperate zone of U.S.
Food: Tender leaves may be cooked. Parboil to remove slight bitter taste. Seeds may be ground and made into cakes or gruel.

13. MARSH MARIGOLD — Brilliant yellow flowers 1" – 1½" across in clusters of one to three. Plant is 1 to 2 feet tall with hollow thick stem. Leaves bright green, rounded or kidney-shaped. Lower leaves long stalked, upper leaves short to no stalk. *Plate 5*
Found: Swamps and damp areas in woods and meadows. Use caution since white hellebore and water hemlock grow in same areas. They are easily distinguishable, providing roots are separated.
Food: Leaves boiled into greens, like spinach. *Do not eat raw!*

14. MAY APPLE — A single flower grows from the forked two-leaf stalks. One umbrella-shaped leaf, which may reach 12" across, grows from each stalk. *Plate 5*
Found: Moist woods.
Food: Caution! Roots of May Apple are poisonous and may cause a skin disease if handled. Pluck only the ripe fruit which follows the flower in early fall.

15. MUSTARD — Smooth-stemmed plant, 1 – 2 feet high with cut and lobed leaves. Yellow, 4-lobed flowers. Seed pods are four-angled. *Plate 5*
Found: All of the U.S. in cultivated fields, along roadsides, etc.
Food: Leaves cooked as a pot-herb and served with butter and vinegar. Flowers may be used as additive to tossed salad and for flavoring other greens.

16. POKEWEED — Tall plants from 4 – 8 feet high. The young, pale green leaves come up in bunches at the base of last year's stalk. Mature plant has red stems. Flowers, small and sometimes tinged with purple, grow in clusters. Dark blue berries follow flowers. *Plate 6*
Found: Fallow fields and in wastelands, along roads, and in forest clearings.
Food: Cut young sprouts when they are 4 – 6 inches high and boil, rinse, and boil again until tender. Cut stem above ground as *roots and berries are poisonous.* Use as an asparagus substitute.

17. PLANTAIN — Long spear-shaped leaves spring from ground on rather coarse stem. Small flowers grow compact on separate stalk and turn into finely grouped seeds. *Plate 6*
Found: Most of U.S. in fields, woods, and lawns.
Food: Early shoots boiled as greens.

18. PURSLANE — A low ground plant. The leaves are juicy, soft, and oval in shape. Normally light green, they may have a red tinge. Its yellow flowers are small and five-petaled. *Plate 6*
Found: Fields, waste places, along streams.
Food: Leaves and stems may be eaten raw. Although slightly sour in taste, they are a good source of water. Leaves and stem may also be cooked by steaming and treated as spinach.

19. SHEEP SORREL OR SOURGRASS — A small herb. Leaves are generally shaped like arrowheads. Dense clusters of reddish flowers are positioned at the top of an erect stalk. *Plate 7*
Found: Dry places.
Food: Leaves can be added sparingly to salad with other less sour greens. Leaves may be eaten raw or stewed, using the resulting juice as a substitute for lemonade.

20. SHEPHERD'S PURSE — A plant growing to about 10 inches. The leaves along the stem are pear-shaped. The lower leaves are deeply and irregularly lobed. Flowers are small and white. *Plate 7*
Found: Fields, waste places.
Food: Young leaves eaten raw or boiled. Tastes somewhat like cabbage.

21. SKUNK CABBAGE — Identified by evil smell. The first flowers appear in the spring even before snow is gone. Grows from 1 – 2 feet tall with lush leaves which appear after the flower which is protected by a spathe or hood. Hood is purplish-brown or greenish-yellow. Masses of scarlet berries appear in the fall. *Plate 7*
Found: Swampy areas in great numbers.
Food: Young shoots and earliest leaves boiled in 2 – 3 changes of water. Roots may be roasted.

22. SOLOMON'S SEAL — Slender stalk with lace-shaped or ovate leaves growing alternately. Flowers grow singly or in twos or threes from leaf axil and are light green, maturing into dark blue berries. *Plate 8*
Found: Stream banks and in moist woods.
Food: The fleshy roots may be boiled or roasted and taste much like parsnips. The young spring shoots are edible also.

23. SPRING BEAUTY — Rather weak stem grows from deep tuber root. Leaves are slender and somewhat fleshy and grow in pairs on the stem. It is one of the earliest spring flowers. Individual flovers all face the same direction and are star-shaped. *Plate 8*
Found: Flood plains or in open woods.
Food: Starchy bulbs are edible either raw or cooked.

24. STINGING NETTLE OR STINGWEED — The leaves grow opposite on a straight stem. The dark green plant has green flower clusters growing from the leaf axil. One has only to brush against this plant to recognize it. It will cause a short-lived but painful stinging sensation. Wear some protection while handling the plant. *Plate 8*
Found: Damp woods and near water.
Food: Add leaves to other boiled greens. Young shoots are similar to bean sprouts. To best obtain these shoots, pull entire plant from ground and remove the shoots. The fiber of the stem, which is also excellent for making rope, will be discussed later.

25. THISTLE — May consist of one or two stalks. growing from 1 – 4 feet high, from dark green to silvery green. Flowers vary in color from pink to purple, white to yellow. *Plate 9*
Found: Fields, pastures, and roadsides.
Food: Remove young plant stalk and leaves, peel stems, and boil until tender.

26. VIOLET — A short plant of many varieties. Varieties show differences in leaf shapes as indicated in sketch. Colors also vary from white to purple. *Plate 9*
Found: Most anywhere.
Food: Leaves, buds, and flowers are edible.

27. WATERCRESS — A plant found in running water with dark green leaves, somewhat rounded. The small flowers are white and may grow individually but usually in clusters. *Plate 9*
Found: Streams, in running water.
Food: Pick leaves and eat raw or add to other greens for added flavor. Use great care in gathering watercress since the deadly water hemlock grows in similar habitats. Also use caution in picking watercress in polluted water.

28. WATER LILY — Rootstock, tubers, and seeds are good raw or cooked. *Plate 10*

29. WILD ONION — A member of the lily family and similar in appearance to the domestic variety. Flat juicy leaves originate from a common point at ground surface. Leaves have strong onion odor. *Plate 10*
Food: Use same as domestic onion. Cooked syrup good for colds. Can be added for seasoning to other greens or meat.

30. WILD RASPBERRY — Is very similar to the domestic raspberry, a shrub which may grow to the height of 3 feet. The stem is prickly and the flowers are small, white, and delicate. *Plate 10*
Found: Open woods, near water, in burned-over areas. They tend to grow in groups or "patches."
Food: Delicious red aggregate berry. Leaves make an excellent tea when boiled for 20 – 25 minutes. Leaves may be dried for later use.

31. WILD ROSE — Similar to domestic rose with delicate five-petal flower varying in color from pink to light-red. *Plate 11*
Found: Open woodlands, meadows, along fences.
Food: Petals added to salad give an excellent taste. The hip may be eaten raw, eat the rind and discard the seeds. Hips may be boiled into jelly by adding sugar and straining seeds.

32. WILD RICE — Tall grass with seed head. *Plate 11*
Found: Swampy streams, rivers, bays, etc.
Food: Lower stem and root shoots are tasty with a sweet flavor. Grain is excellent in fall.

33. **WILD STRAWBERRY** — Leaves from medium to dark green with small white flowers and red fruit. *Plate 11*
Found: Fields, meadows, roadsides, woods.
Food: Berries rich in vitamin A. Leaves may be boiled for tea.

34. **WOOD SORREL** — Leaves are clover-like growing in a tuft directly from a small brown bulb. Flowers grow in clusters of various sizes from the top of a slender stalk. *Plate 12*
Found: Dry woods. Found nearly worldwide.
Food: Although leaves have an acid taste, they are not unpleasant. Tubers of some varieties are also eaten.

35. **YUCCA** — A large plant with broad rigid leaves terminating in sharp, thorny points. Leaves originate from base of flower stalk. The flowers are white and cup-shaped, clustered toward the top of the stem. The fruit is green or yellow. *Plate 12*
Found: Plains, hillsides, in dry soil with plenty of sunlight.
Food: Flowers eaten raw. The fruit can be stewed. Stalk can be cut into sections and boiled. Fruit can also be baked and eaten after fibres are removed. Also baked fruit can be pounded, water added and boiled into thick paste, rolled into sheets and eaten or sun-dried and preserved for later meals.

36. **JOSHUA TREE** — Treelike in growth, often reaching 30 feet high with stout trunk and boldly forked branches. Leaves are stiff and sharply pointed. Stalks of large waxy greenish flowers appear March – May. *Plate 12*
Found: Very dry land.
Food: Seeds edible. Flowers roasted on hot coals have high sugar content.

37. **JACK-IN-THE-PULPIT (Indian Turnip)** — A perennial which may grow for one to three feet in height, the latter being most common. Two petioled leaves are sheathed with the flower stalk. Each leaf has three ovate, pointed leaflets. A round club-shaped spadix two to three inches long is situated at the top of the flower stalk. Surrounding the spadix is a green and purple striped spathe ending in a flap over the top. Flowers change to green and produce bright red berries in the fall. *Plate 13*
Found: Rich, low woods mostly where soil is moist.
Food: Bulb boiled in many changes of water. Suggest boiling and then drying after which bulb can be pounded into meal.

38. PRAIRIE TURNIP (Wild potato, Indian Bread Root) — Erect stalk 6 to 15 inches high with few branches. Stems covered with soft hairs. Leaves composed of 5 obovate leaflets tapering toward the base. Flowers are purplish blue. *Plate 13*
Found: Prairies and high plains.
Food: Can be peeled and eaten raw, boiled or roasted. May be cut into strips and dried for later use or pounded into meal.

39. GROUNDNUT — A smooth slender climbing vine with milky juice, growing 5 – 10 feet long. Root system consists of a number of tubers connected with fibrous strands. Leaves are compound with 5 – 7 ovate leaflets. Flowers are brownish purple. Resulting pods resemble those of the bean. *Plate 13*
Found: Mainly in low damp soil.
Food: Tubers are sweet and edible. May be eaten raw, boiled or roasted. One of our best wild foods.

40. CHUFA (Nut Grass, Earth Almond) — Grass-like plants with basal leaves, a strong stalk 1 – 2 feet tall and a circle of leaves at the top below flower clusters of yellow spikelets. *Plate 14*
Found: Cultivated or waste land in damp soil.
Food: Tubers edible.

41. FALSE SOLOMONS SEAL — Grows 1 – 3 feet tall. Stems solitary, leafy, and often zigzagged. Leaves alternate lance-shaped or elliptical, wavy at edges. *Plate 14*
Found: Moist woods often together with true Solomons Seal.
Food: Rootstocks edible after cooking. Young shoots also edible. Berries which follow flowers are edible but cathartic and should be avoided.

42. WILD GINGER — Two kidney-shaped or heart-shaped leaves on separate stems appear in spring. Grows to height of 5 – 10 inches. Stems covered with fine hair. The single brownish purple flower appears on a short stem between the leaf stems. *Plate 14*
Found: Rich soil in woodlands.
Food: Dried or fresh roots used as substitute for ginger.

PLATE I

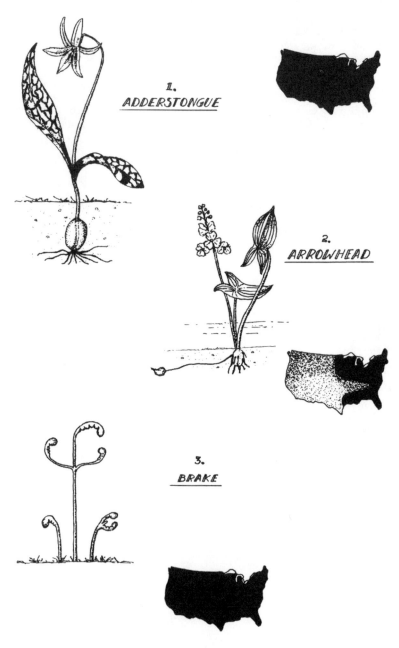

1.
ADDERSTONGUE

2.
ARROWHEAD

3.
BRAKE

PLATE 2

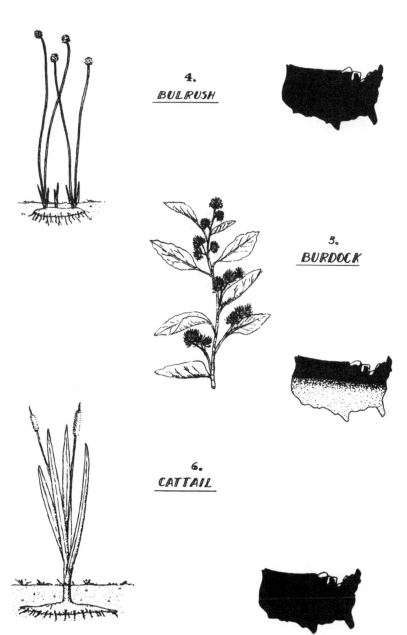

4.
BULRUSH

5.
BURDOCK

6.
CATTAIL

PLATE 3

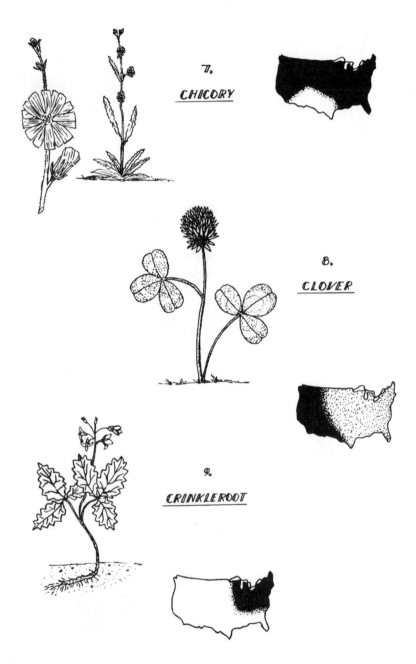

7.

CHICORY

8.

CLOVER

9.

CRINKLEROOT

PLATE 4

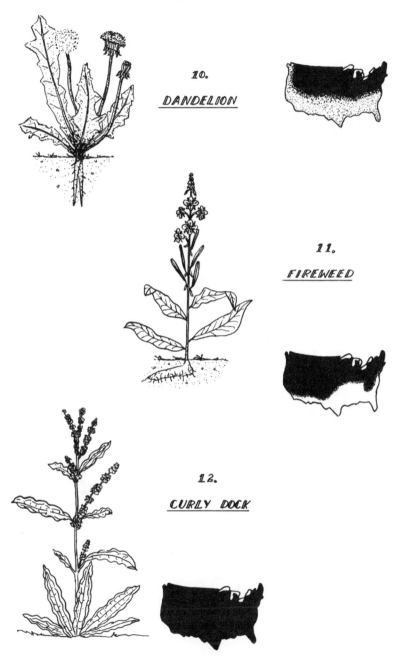

10.

DANDELION

11.

FIREWEED

12.

CURLY DOCK

PLATE 5

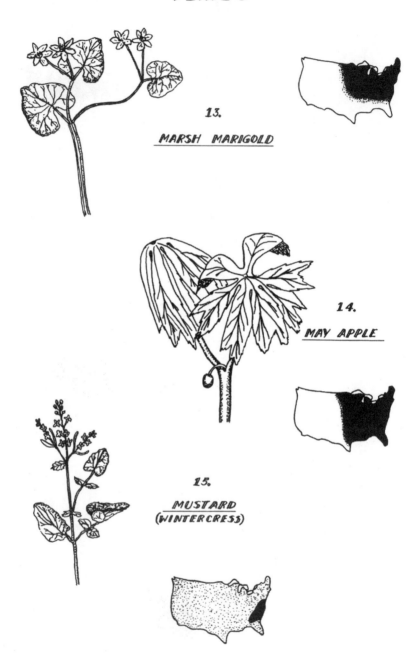

13.

MARSH MARIGOLD

14.

MAY APPLE

15.

MUSTARD
(WINTERCRESS)

PLATE 6

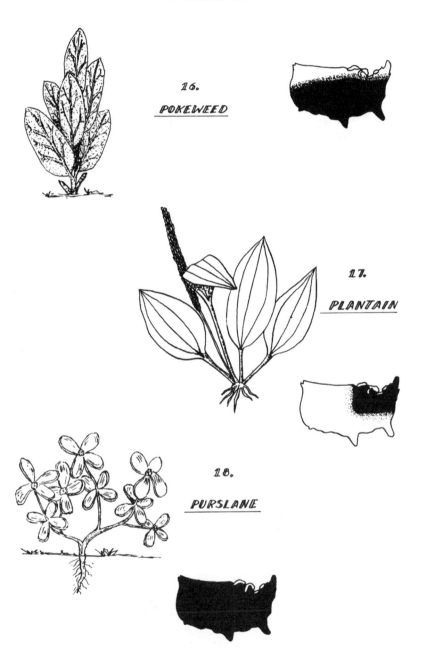

16.

POKEWEED

17.

PLANTAIN

18.

PURSLANE

PLATE 7

19.

SHEEP SORREL

20.

SHEPHERD'S PURSE

21.

SKUNK CABBAGE

PLATE 8

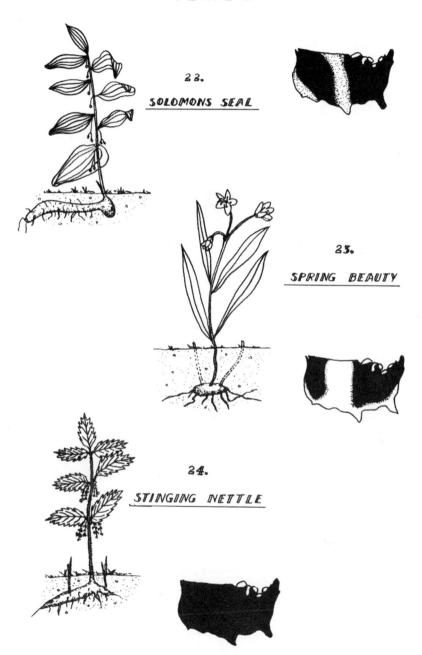

22.

SOLOMONS SEAL

23.

SPRING BEAUTY

24.

STINGING NETTLE

PLATE 9

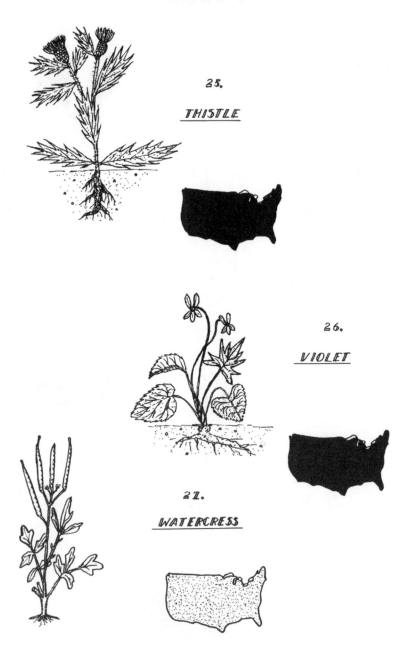

25.

THISTLE

26.

VIOLET

27.

WATERCRESS

PLATE 10

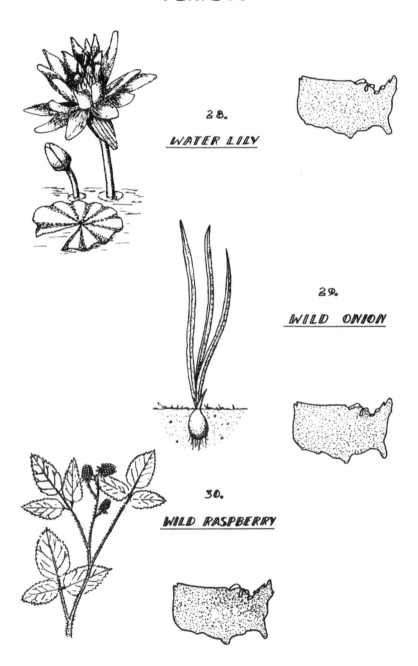

28.

WATER LILY

29.

WILD ONION

30.

WILD RASPBERRY

PLATE II

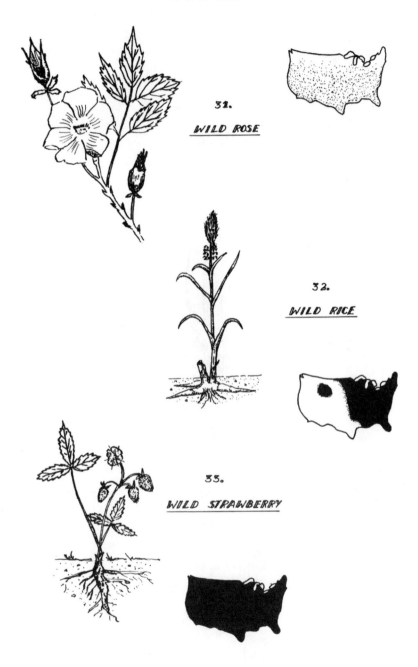

31.

WILD ROSE

32.

WILD RICE

33.

WILD STRAWBERRY

PLATE 12

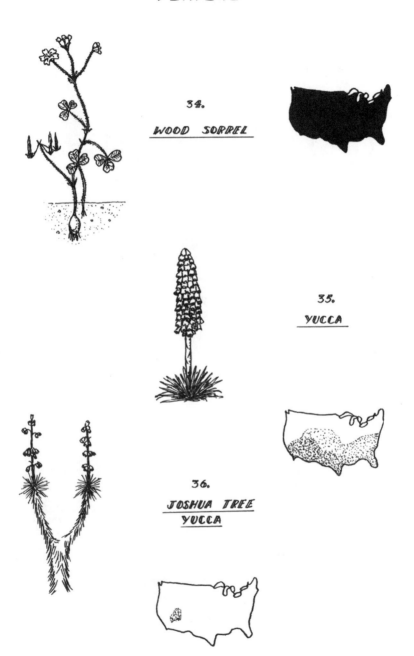

34.

WOOD SORREL

35.

YUCCA

36.

JOSHUA TREE
YUCCA

PLATE 13

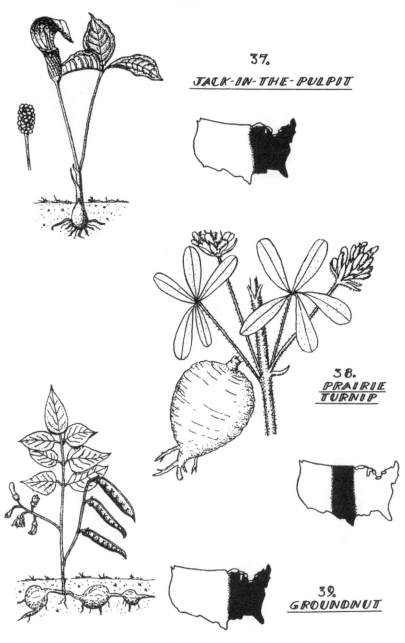

37.
JACK-IN-THE-PULPIT

38.
PRAIRIE
TURNIP

39.
GROUNDNUT

PLATE 14

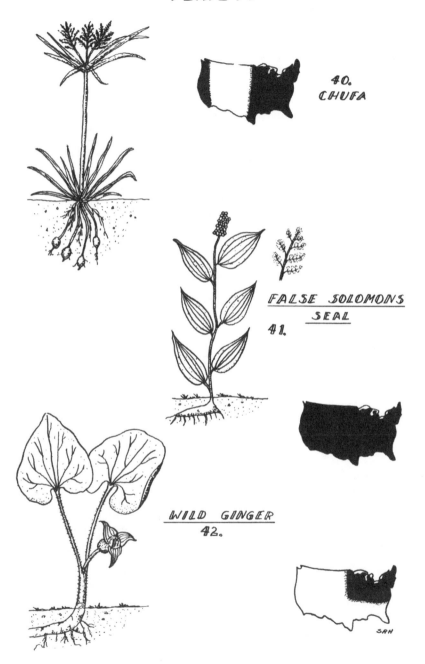

40.
CHUFA

FALSE SOLOMONS
SEAL
41.

WILD GINGER
42.

FOOD TREES
Plate 15

1. HAWTHORN — A small tree with many thorns an inch long. Leaves are toothed.
Found: Much of the U.S.
Food: Red fruit in fall is edible, better if cooked with added sugar.

2. OAK — The acorn can be eaten if tannin is removed by leaching.
Food: Boil acorns in many changes of water until "yellow" is gone from water or cook with wood ash for an hour and then rinse.

3. SUMAC — Pithy-twigged shrubs rarely growing over 20 feet in height. May form thickets. STAGHORN SUMAC — Hairy twigs and leaves, almost white beneath. DWARF SUMAC — Much smaller leafstalk between the leaves is winged.
Food: The staghorn and dwarf sumac flowers may be boiled, sugar added, and made into a lemonade substitute.

4. BOX ELDER — May grow 50 feet in height. Its leaves grow oppositely on green twigs with 3 – 5 large, coarse toothed leaflets. Member of maple family.
Food: Collect sap in spring and make syrup. Takes 10 – 12 hours of patience.

5. WILD PLUM — Usually classified as a shrub. They form thickets through eastern half of U.S. Leaves are rounder and coarser than those of the cherry. Fruit grows singly and is orange or red when ripe.
Food: Eat fruit raw or cooked.

6. PIN CHERRY — Small slender tree rarely growing more than 30 feet in height and found in eastern half of U.S. and in the mountains. Bark is rusty-brown and marked with large lenticels or ventilating pores. Leaves are thick, narrow, taper to a long point, and are finely toothed. Fruit is red when ripe and grows in clusters.
Food: Eat fruit raw or cooked.

7. PINON — Small pine of dryer mountainous regions. Grows from 15 – 50 feet in height. Needles in two or threes although one variety has needles singly. Needles ¾" to 1" long. The seeds extracted from the cones are delicious.

8. BASSWOOD — Grows to height of from 60 – 100 feet. Grayish-brown twigs bear plump winter buds. Leaves are veiny, heart-shaped, and large.
Food: Sap contains considerable sugar. The basswood fruit ground with some of the flowers furnishes a paste which in texture and taste perfectly resembles chocolate. Flowers used as a substitute for tea.

9. **SERVICE BERRY** — A tree or shrub. Oblong, or roundish, sharply or coarsely toothed, slender stalked alternate leaves. Bark is smooth, grayish. Flowers and fruits in elongated drooping clusters.
Found: Woods, swamps, open fields.
Food: Cooked for sauces, raw or dried.

10. **JUNIPERS** — Grows 15 – 60 feet in height. Stout spreading trees with thin, scaly or fibrous bark. Leaves are blunt and scaly, growing close to the twig. Berries are bluish.
Found: Rocky, sandy or other poor soil.
Food: Food seasoning, use either fresh or dried.

PLATE 15

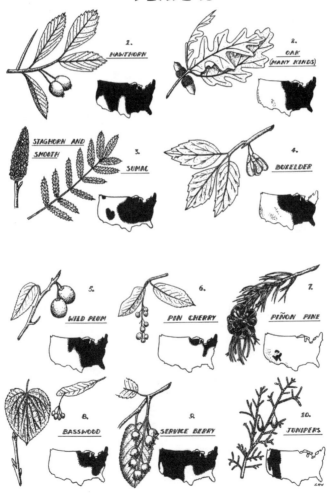

MENU AT A GLANCE

Most areas have a number of edible wild plants. The following list summarizes the various varieties and their most common uses as food.

I. Tubers
Chufa
Groundnut
Water Lily
Wood Sorrel

II. Roots
Braken Fern
Bulrush
Burdock
Cattail
Chicory
Crinkleroot
Dandelion
False Solomons Seal
Skunk Cabbage
Solomons Seal
Water Lily
Wild Ginger

III. Bulbs
Adderstongue
Arrowhead
Jack-in-the-pulpit
Prairie Turnip
Spring Beauty
Wild Onion

IV. Shoots
Bulrush
Cattail
Fireweed
Pokeweed
Skunk Cabbage
Solomons Seal
Thistle

V. Stems
Bulrush
Burdock
Clover
Purslane
Thistle
Yucca

VI. Berries and Fruits
Hawthorn
Juniper
May Apple
Oak
Pin Cherry
Service Berry
Wild Plum
Wild Raspberry
Yucca

VII. Flowers and Buds
Basswood
Clover
Joshua Tree
Rose
Sumac
Violet
Yucca

VIII. Leaves
Adderstongue
Braken Fern
Chicory
Curly Dock
Dandelion
Fireweed
Marsh Marigold
Mustard
Nettle
Plantain
Purslane
Sheep Sorrel
Shepherd's Purse
Violet
Watercress
Wild Onion
Wild Raspberry
Wild Strawberry

IX. Seeds
Clover
Curly Dock
Joshua Tree

Pinon
Water Lily
Wild Rice

X. Sap for Sugar
Box Elder
Basswood

XI. Drinks
Sheep Sorrel – Lemonade
Raspberry – Tea
Strawberry – Tea
Sumac – Lemonade
Box Elder – Tea
Basswood – Tea
Chicory – Coffee

XII. Seasoning
Cattail
Juniper
Rose
Wild Ginger
Wild Onion

64

PEMMICAN

Pemmican is probably the best known and most remembered of all American Indian foods. Extensive use by the Indians accounts for the adoption of pemmican by early explorers. It was used not necessarily as an every day food, but rather as a fill-in and also in emergencies when fresh food was scarce and when time and/or circumstances limited foraging and preparation of fresh varieties.

A Cree word meaning mixture, pemmican was made of a combination of dried buffalo meat pounded into a sort of flour and dried berries blended with melted fat. The mix was stored in skin bags and remained usable for many months.

A modern pemmican may be made in the field providing time is available for proper drying and preparation of ingredients. Prepare several pounds of meat by cutting into thin strips and hanging in the sun to dry. When the strips reach a point closely resembling pieces of leather, pound into "flour." Smoked meat may also be used if well cured.

Assuming that no sugar is available, there are a number of substitutes which may be used. Maple or birch sap may be boiled down as can the blossoms of the milkweed. The root of the bulrush will also yield a sweet syrup if the root is lacerated and boiled. If sugar is available, preferably brown, add ½ cup.

Raisins are most generally the fruit used. However, any type of dried berry can be substituted in an emergency. Dried wild onion, leech, and crushed seeds may also be added in small amounts to improve body and flavor.

After all ingredients have been mixed, add several pounds of melted suet and blend. Store in skin bag or in a cloth bag sealed with paraffin or wax. It may be eaten raw, fried or added to water to make a thick gruel.

Fresh pemmican, properly made, is not unpleasant but grows more tasteless as it ages. As a suggestion, suspend your pemmican in a cloth bag and smoke it slowly for several days. This will enhance the flavor and aid in preservation.

POISONOUS PLANTS

1. Water Hemlock — Heavily scented herbs of the parsley family. Seven species are found in the U.S. At least one variety grows in most areas of U.S., especially in swamps, wet meadows, and along ditches. The plant may grow to a height of 7 feet. Leaves are small and pinnately compound. Flowers are white and occur in terminal compound umbels. The leaves, and particularly the roots which resemble parsnips, contain a deadly alkaloid, cicutoxin, which may easily be fatal to humans and livestock. *Plate 17*

Symptoms of poisoning: Stomach pain, nausea, diarrhea, dilated pupils, frothing at the mouth.

Treatment: Give emetic followed by cathartic.

2. Buttercup — Most of the 40 species in the U.S. grow widely in low moist places. Some varieties are creepers but most are erect and branching with hairy stems and deeply lobed leaves. Flower petals are skinny, butter yellow, and very occasionally white, enclosing many stamens. Plants contain a volatile acid called anemenol, often strong enough to raise blisters on the skin. Severe inflammation of the intestine may result from eating. Since the acid is volatile, it can be driven off by drying. *Plate 16*

3. False Hellebore — All perennial plants of the lily family, growing 2 – 8 feet tall. Leaves are broad and deeply veined. The flowers are somewhat star-shaped, greenish, yellowish or purple, in handsome spikes that bloom from June to August. The plants are most usually found in damp and marshy areas, primarily in the higher mountains and along the Pacific Coast. Although the foliage is fatal to cattle, the poison is concentrated in the roots. The poison contains alkaloids of jervine, veratrine, and cevaline. *Plate 16*

Symptoms of poisoning: Abdominal pain, muscular weakness, general paralysis, muscular spasms, infrequent then rapid pulse.

4. White Baneberry — The white baneberry is a hardy member of the crowfoot family. The leaves are deeply toothed leaflets. The white flowers grow in clusters at the top of the flower stalk, producing berries in the fall. Berries are white, black tipped, and are the most poisonous part of the plant. Some variety in most of U.S. *Plate 16*

Symptoms of poisoning: Increased pulse, dizziness, burning stomach.

Treatment: Give emetic.

5. Larkspur — Over 100 varieties in the United States, primarily from the Great Plains to the Pacific Coast. They are erect annual or perennial herbs growing from one to five or six feet in height. Leaves are divided with branching stems and flower on a terminal spike. Flowers range from blue and purple to red. Most varieties have poison delphinine in the foliage, flowers, seeds, and roots. *Plate 16*
Symptoms of poisoning: Loss of appetite, constipation.
Treatment: Vomiting.

6. Jimson Weed — The jimson weed is a coarse, rank smelling herb — a very poisonous member of the nightshade family. Found growing in waste areas, it is a strong plant with a strong stem growing from one to five feet in height. Widespread in U.S., especially in the South. The leaves are broad and irregularly lobed. The funnel-shaped white or violet flowers grow up to four inches long. The seeds are encased in a prickly, ovoid seed capsule. A very potent narcotic drug, hyoscyamine, is found in the leaves and seeds. *Plate 17*
Symptoms of poisoning: Headache, nausea, vertigo, extreme thirst, loss of sight, convulsion, and death.
Treatment: Vomiting and cathartic.

7. Monkshood — An extremely poisonous member of the crowroot family. The plant which grows from two to five feet in height is native to the Northern Hemisphere with four species occurring in the United States and Canada. A powerful diaphoretic and analgesic drug called aconitine is concentrated primarily in the roots and seeds and occasionally in the flowers. Some species of the monkshood are grown as garden perennials. The tall stalks contain helmet-shaped yellow, blue, white, and occasionally bicolored flowers. *Plate 17*
Symptoms of poisoning: Muscular weakness, irregular and labored breathing, weak pulse, bloating.

8. Milkweed — There are some 60 varieties of milkweed in the United States, a tall plant growing from two to five feet in height. All parts of the plant contain a milky juice and grow in old fields, meadows, and marshes in abundance. The leaves grow opposite each other and the large seed pods are arranged in pairs. The broad flower clusters are orange, red to pink, lilac, and creamy white. Several Western varieties are exceedingly poisonous. *Plate 17*
Symptoms of poisoning: Loss of muscular control, staggering, violent spasms, rapid and weak pulse, respiratory paralysis.

PLATE 16

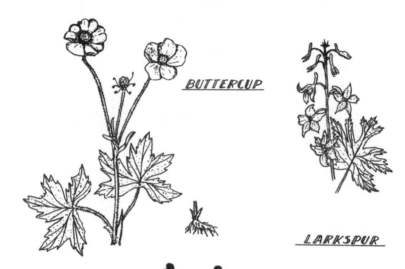

BUTTERCUP

LARKSPUR

PLANTS SHOWN ARE POISONOUS AND
SHOULD BE AVOIDED.

WHITE BANEBERRY

FALSE HELLEBORE

PLATE 17

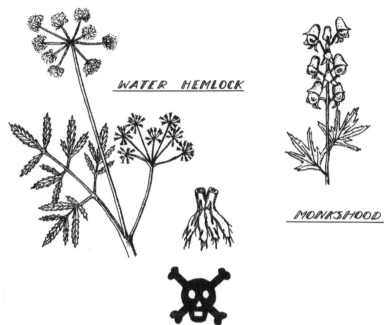

WATER HEMLOCK

MONKSHOOD

PLANTS SHOWN ARE POISONOUS AND
SHOULD BE AVOIDED.

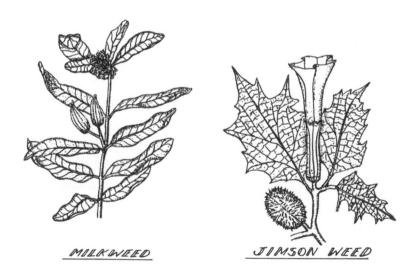

MILKWEED

JIMSON WEED

FUNGUS FOODS

Although fungi afford some extremely delicious foods, some of their number are deadly poisoners. Although numerous tests have been devised to distinguish the edible from the poisonous varieties, tests have proven only that no foolproof tests are possible.

It is well to note that some fungi are so deadly that a few spores may prove fatal. In some instances, no remedy is known.

Examine page 74 carefully. Learn the distinguishing nomenclature and the important rules regarding mushrooms.

EDIBLE MUSHROOMS

There are a few fungi which are safe for amateurs.

1. **Inky Coprinus** — So called because at maturity the caps melt away into an inky fluid. This mushroom is tall and delicate and has a grayish or a grayish-brown cap. The gills are a dark gray. There are no poisonous black-spored mushrooms in the United States. *Plate 18*

2. **Morel Mushrooms** — Sometimes called a sponge mushroom because of its sponge-like appearance. All members of the family are edible. They appear the earliest each year, usually appearing in May and June. Their strange appearance will make them easy to identify. A morel mushroom resembles a sponge on a stem. *Plate 18*

3. **Coral Fungus** — Resembles sea coral and may vary in color from white to yellow, tan or violet. The coral mushroom should be picked young as they grow tough with age. *Plate 19*

4. **Puffball** — So very easy to identify, these range from pea-size to 16 – 18 inches with some growing much larger. No puffballs are poisonous. They should be taken young while still firm and white. When cut, they resemble cheese. When mature, they break into a mass of brown spores.
   If when you cut it open the puffball is not solid but rather shows any type of embryo structure, it is not a puffball but a "button" or immature mushroom and should not be eaten.
   Large puffballs may have slices cut from them. The cut will heal and growth will continue. *Plate 19*

5. **Beefsteak Mushroom** — Resembles a piece of raw beefsteak as the name implies. It is blood red, soft, and juicy. It is found on wounds on oak and chestnut trees about midsummer, also on chestnut stumps. The mushroom is often 6 – 8 inches across. *Plate 18*

Other types of edible mushrooms:
1. Meadow or Pasture
2. Shaggy Mane
3. Glistening Coprinus
4. Fairy Ring
5. Oyster
6. Elm
7. Orange Milk
8. Hypomyces Laclifluorum
9. Perplexing Hypholoma
10. Chanterelle
11. Graylings
12. Sulphur
13. Hedgehog
14. Coral
15. Greenish Russula

Consult an expert when attempting to identify edible types!

POISONOUS MUSHROOMS
(Plates 20 & 21)

1. Deadly Amanita
This poisonous variety is pleasant to view and varies in color from white to green, olive and grayish-brown. The surface is smooth and if moist, becomes rather sticky.

Identifiable points are white gills, cup, hollow stem, ruff, and gills free from the stem.

The poisonous substance in the amanita is phaelin, an alcohol-id similar to snake venom which dissolves the blood corpuscles.

2. Fly Amanita
Similar to the deadly amanita but may also be found in colors from yellow to orange to red. Cap has raised white spots. The poison is muscarin which reacts similarly to phaelin.

Other types of poisonous mushrooms:
1. Common Entoloma
2. Green-Spored Mushroom
3. Emetic Russula
4. Fetid Russula
5. Large-Sheathed Amanitopsio
6. Jack-O-Lantern
7. Common Stinkhorn

PLATE 18

INKY
COPRINUS

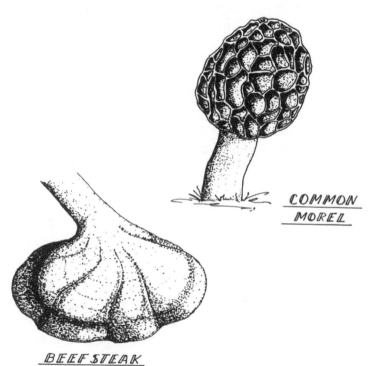

COMMON
MOREL

BEEF STEAK
FUNGUS

PLATE 19

CORAL FUNGUS

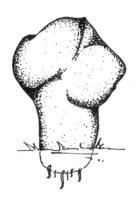

PUFFBALLS

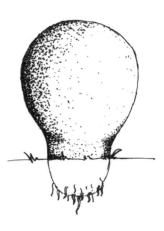

GENERAL INFORMATION ON MUSHROOMS

ALL MUSHROOMS ARE FUNGI BUT ALL FUNGI ARE NOT MUSHROOMS.
FUNGI AFFORD SOME DELICIOUS FOOD AND SOME DEADLY POISONERS.
TESTS HAVE PROVEN ONLY THAT NO FOOLPROOF METHOD IS KNOW
TO DISTINGUISH EDIBLE FROM POISONOUS FUNGI.
   LEARN TERMINOLOGY AND RULES ON THIS AND FOLLOWING PAGES.

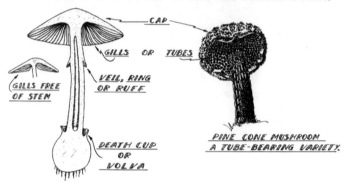

PINE CONE MUSHROOM
A TUBE-BEARING VARIETY.

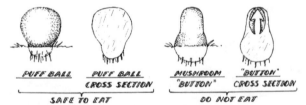

A FEW BASIC RULES FOR THE AMATEUR:

1. DON'T PICK MUSHROOM WITH RUFF OR VEIL.
2. DON'T PICK MUSHROOM WHOSE STEM COMES FROM CUP OR VOLVA.
3. DON'T PICK MUSHROOM HAVING MILKY JUICE.
4. DON'T PICK BUTTONS.
5. DON'T PICK FUNGI SHOWING SIGNS OF DECAY.
6. DON'T PICK YELLOW OR WHITE GILLED MUSHROOMS.
7. DON'T PICK TUBE-BEARING VARIETIES.
8. DON'T PICK FUNGI THAT CHANGE COLOR WHEN INJURED.
9. DON'T EAT MUSHROOMS WITH A PEPPERY TASTE.
10. DON'T PICK FUNGI WITH GILLS FREE OF STEM.

REMEMBER — DON'T TAKE CHANCES!!

SRH

PLATE 20

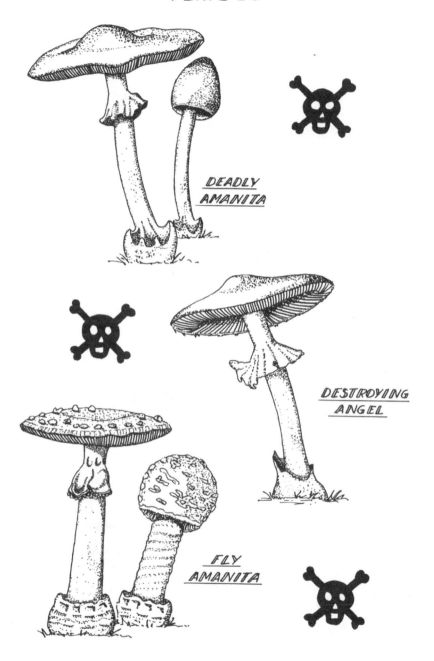

DEADLY
AMANITA

DESTROYING
ANGEL

FLY
AMANITA

PLATE 21

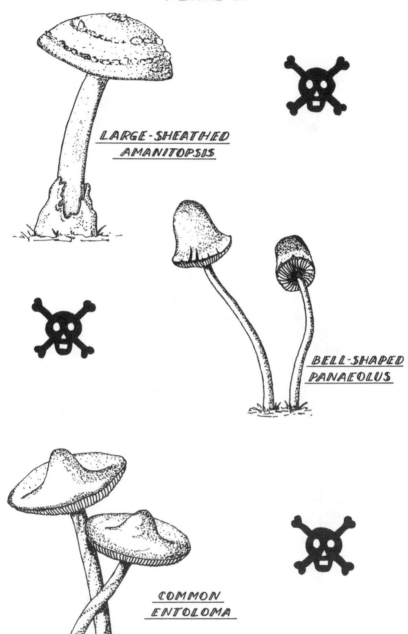

LARGE-SHEATHED
AMANITOPSIS

BELL-SHAPED
PANAEOLUS

COMMON
ENTOLOMA

MEDICINAL PLANTS
(Plates 22 – 26)

Wilderness or survival first aid at first glance would seem very restrictive in scope since it would probably be presumed that without a medical kit very little could be done to minimize physical discomfort and/or improve health during a survival ordeal.

Through the years, I have picked up bits and pieces of information pertaining to the subject. Some of that material has been used herein while much more was discarded as valueless.

When setting out to compile this information, I concluded that one fundamental way to begin would be to make a list of some basic American Indian "cure-alls." I recognized that there was a considerable list but further realized that probably a great number had no scientific basis for consideration or had harmful or questionable characteristics.

In checking my library, I found that the 33rd annual report of the *Bureau of American Ethnology*, Smithsonian Institute, 1911 – 1912, included an excellent report on the use of plants by the Indians in the Missouri River basin. I went through each item — both plants and trees — listing those which had even the remotest possibility of possessing properties which would make them useable either in external or internal first aid, providing that care and discretion were used in application.

To this list I added a number of miscellaneous plants and trees from a variety of other written and oral sources. The list when compiled included 84 items.

Since I felt that no item should be included which had noticeable poisonous or questionable characteristics, each was checked first against Muenscher's *Poisonous Plants of the United States*. Those which he listed as poisonous in any form were eliminated from the list. Secondly, the remaining list was checked item for item in the *Dispensatory of the United States of America*, 25th edition. Again, those plants which although not poisonous appeared to have little basis for consideration or possessed some possibly questionable characteristics were eliminated.

When those eliminations were completed, only 19 of the original selections remained. Although the final list, which is included herein, represents only a small number of potentially useful plants to be found in North America, they do include remedies and aids in the following categories.

1. Cuts and bruises
2. Stomach upset
3. Constipation
4. Diarrhea
5. Colds
6. Sore throat
7. Insect bites
8. Poison ivy
9. Skin rash
10. Sunburn
11. Sprains
12. Coughs
13. Sore eyes
14. Ear ache
15. Tooth ache

As mentioned elsewhere, wilderness survival is not an easy procedure or a pleasant experience, regardless of how much one may think he knows about the wilderness or how well one might be prepared emotionally and physically.

Hopefully, rescue or finding one's way out will be accomplished in two or three days. Under such circumstances very few survival first aid techniques need be of concern.

However, how does one predict the duration of the experience and/or the problems to be encountered?

Obviously, the longer the duration, the more important it becomes to be aware of a variety of survival techniques to aid in the struggle to stay alive and well.

More than likely, survival circumstances will magnify physical discomforts since everyday medications usually so accessible and so normally used are absent.

Heat, sun, lack of food, emotional stress, dampness, and insects in the rawest forms will compound the problem.

Nature's many gifts — ours for the taking providing we are willing to work for them — include a variety of medicinal items. Few can be expected to work miracles, but they all have value and merit your consideration.

In discussing this list of medicinal plants and their uses, the following glossary of terms will be used.

Antiscorbutics — Preparations used to combat scurvy, a lack of vitamin C.

Antiseptic — A plant product which will oppose the growth or cause destruction of germs.

Astringent — Plant substances which contract body tissue and slow or stop the flow of blood.

Carminative — Relieves stomach gas.

Cathartic — Relief for constipation.

Constipation — See cathartic.

Decoction — Medicines made from plants by simmering in water since boiling can destroy helpful properties. Strain before using.

Demulcents — Plant products used to soothe the intestinal tract.

Diarrhea — Unnatural and profuse intestinal discharge.

Emetic — Plants which cause vomiting.

Emollient — A softening or soothing agent.

Expectorants — Substances that assist in expelling phlegm.

Infusion — Plants ground or powdered and mixed in warm water.

Styptic — Plant properties which cause blood vessels to contract.

WILDERNESS FIRST AID
Potentially A Survival Problem!

HOW WOULD YOU TREAT---

CUTS Sore Eyes ?
Sprains
? TOOTH ACHE constipation
COLDS ? TENSION
Coughs poisoning insect bites heat exhaustion BRUISES
Diarrhea EAR stomach upset
poison ivy ACHE
? sore throat SUNBURN ?

79

PLATE 22

Flowering Dogwood

Description: The simple leaves with nearly parallel veins are oppositely located on the branches. The flower is actually a group of enlarged bracts (leaves), pink in color, around a small true flower. The wood is dense and compact.

Found: Many varieties found in most areas of the U.S.

Use: Bark boiled in water will produce an astringent. Use also for external cuts and as gargle for sore mouth. Large doses used as a cathartic.

Bonset: Eupatorium Perfoliatum

Description: Bonset has been used interchangeably with Joepyeweed (epatorium purpureum), a member of the same compositae family. Growing 3 – 4 feet in height with hairy opposite leaves, the stem comes up through the leaves. Flowers are white.

Found: Eastern half U.S.

Use: Upper leaves and flowers are dried and rubbed into coarse powder. Add one spoonful of powder to one pint water and use for cold relief; drink about ½ cup every few hours. Large doses used as an emetic.

Alder: Alnus Rugosa

Description: Close relatives of the birches with seeds, fruits, and flowers very similar. Usually only shrubs however. Bark appears much the same as the birches. Leaves are short stemmed and alternate with strong veins.

Found: There are 8 varieties of alder in the United States. The European, black, speckled, and hazel alder range west to the Mississippi River. The red, thin-leaf, white, and mountain varieties range westward from the Rocky Mountains.

Use: Bark contains large amounts of tannin used for the astringent qualities. May be used for cuts and bruises and as a gargle. Leaves if crushed may be used as a poultice in treating skin rashes.

Wild Onion: Garlic

Description: Similar to cultured onion. Identified by smell.

Found: Nearly entire U.S.

Use: Widely recognized for medicinal qualities. The juice is antiseptic. A syrup made from with water in which bulbs were boiled (adding sugar if available) is excellent for colds, sore throat, and hoarseness. Great addition for flavoring food.

PLATE 22

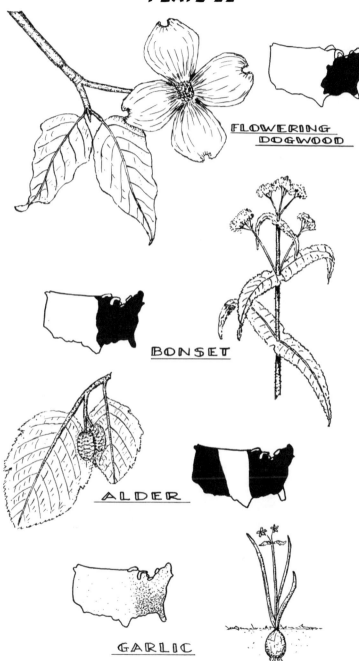

FLOWERING
DOGWOOD

BONSET

ALDER

GARLIC

PLATE 23

Slippery Elm: Ulmus Rubra

Description: A lofty tree, 40 to 70 feet in height, with short trunk 15 to 20 inches in diameter and spreading branches which are rough and whitish. The bark is dark brown, often with a tinge of red, cracked into rough ridges. The inner bark is white and very mucilaginous. The leaves are 1 – 7 inches long, ovate-oblong, pale green, very rough on top with unequally serrated edges. The fruit has smooth wings and a hairy center.

Found: North of the Carolinas, west of the Allegheny Mountains, west to the Dakotas, and north to Western Quebec and Lake Huron. Prefers higher dry, firm soil.

Use: The mucilaginous inner bark was boiled in water as a folk remedy for coughs and diarrhea. Powdered inner bark mixed with water was also an excellent emollient for application in cases of external inflammation.

Paper, White or Canoe Birch: Betula Papyrifern

Description: Most widely distributed of birches, may reach 60 to 70 feet in height, 2 – 3 feet in diameter but usually smaller. The outer bark is creamy white and peels easily. The inner bark shows shades of orange. The leaves are 1 – 4 inches long, ovate, narrowed or rounded at the base, irregularly toothed, dull green, usually smooth above and slightly hairy beneath on veins. Pollen producing flowers grow in erect cone-like clusters which become drooping tassels.

Found: Ranges from Atlantic coast to Iowa and north nearly to the Hudson Bay into Labrador and Newfoundland.

Use: Young shoots and leaves secrete a resinous substance which is said to be laxative if taken in quanity. The inner bark is bitter and has astringent qualities. The leaves are aromatic. Birch tea is good for general body ache and as a carminative.

Wild Cherry (Choke Cherry): Prunus Virginiana

Description: Shrub or small tree, usually growing not more than 20 feet high. Oval leaves are 2 – 4 inches long, about half as wide, pointed, with saw-toothed edges. Bark is smooth, dull brown or grayish and forms irregular curved scales in older trees. Flowers appear when leaves are about mature. Pea-sized fruit in drooping clusters are yellow to nearly black and ripen late in July to August.

Found: Fourteen varieties throughout most of the U.S. and into Canada.

Use: Bark boiled in water and used for coughs. However, the mix is of questionable value and should be used in minimal amounts.

Prickly Pear: Opuntia Humifusa

Description: Thick-jointed branching plant may grow 1 inch high but usually is prostrate. Joints are oval and 2" – 5" long. Bristles are reddish brown. Flowers are yellow — usually with red center — about 3" in diameter with 10 to 12 petals. The fruit, about 1½" – 2" long and about as thick, is filled with purplish pulp which is edible.

Found: In sandy soil, Ohio to Michigan, Minnesota, and Texas.

Use: Peel the stem and hold over bruise or wound. It is good because of the mucilaginous properties it possesses. Also used as a packing for sprains and as a relief for insect bites.

PLATE 23

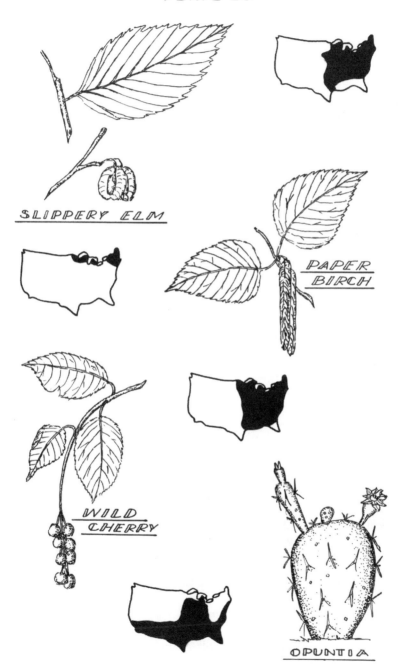

SLIPPERY ELM

PAPER BIRCH

WILD CHERRY

OPUNTIA

PLATE 24

Witch Hazel: Hammamelis Virginiana

Description: A study shrub or small tree related to the sweet gum. Height may vary from 5' to 15', occasionally reaching 25'. Bark is brown and smooth, but scaly on old trees. The leaves are 2" – 6" long and broad and uneven at the base, oval to roundish. The margin is irregularly wavy or coarsely toothed. Top side of the leaf is usually smooth, hairy on veins beneath. Yellow flowers appear in the fall as the leaves begin to fall. The fruit is a woody, hairy pod splitting into two parts as flowers appear.

Found: Found most frequently in low, rich soil but also grows well in rocky banks. It ranges from Florida to Texas and north from Minnesota to Nova Scotia. The southern variety has rough leaves covered with hairs on the upper surface, and the leaves are 3" – 5" long. It is found from Georgia to Florida, west to Texas and Arkansas, doing especially well in Alabama and Louisiana.

Use: A strong solution made from the bark mades a good poultice for sores and bruises. Its astringent qualities are also good for cuts and abrasions. I have seen references which indicate that finely powdered bark may be inhaled to combat nosebleed. This seems logical but since I've not had powdered bark and a nosebleed simultaneously, I cannot speak authoritatively.

Calamus (Sweet Flag, Sweet Root, Sweet Cane): Acorus Calamus

Description: A perennial herb of the Aram family which resembles the iris. Fleshy rootstocks grow in masses many feet long. It has sword-shaped leaves like the iris but yellow-green and shiny, 2' long or longer in many instances. The leaf is 1" wide, sharp edged with prominent mid-vein. Leaves sheath each other at the base. The spadix or flower head, about halfway up the stem, bears tiny yellow-green flowers.

Found: Found over the eastern half of the United States.

Use: For indigestion and digestive stimulant, the spadix may be eaten raw. Roots may be peeled and chewed for coughs. The roots may also be candied as a confection. I also found reference that the powdered root is highly valued as an insecticide in India and Ceylon. I have no verification of this at the time of writing.

Pennyroyal (Mosquito plant, Squaw Mint): Hedeoma Pulegioides

Description: Annual plant from 9" – 15" high with a small branching fibrous yellow root, quadrangular stem and numerous branches which are slender and erect. Tiny blue flowers cluster in the upper leaf axils.

Found: Common in eastern and midwestern United States, preferring dry ground.

Use: Dried leaves are aromatic. Mildly stimulating drink infusion taken in small doses for upset stomach.

PLATE 24

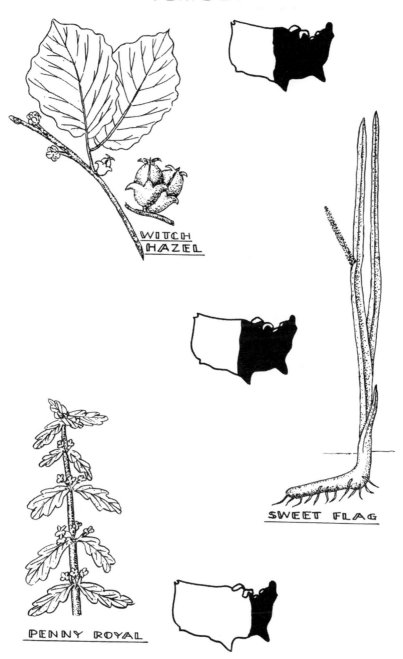

WITCH
HAZEL

SWEET FLAG

PENNY ROYAL

PLATE 25

Pine: Various varieties.

Use: As an inhalant; chop needles and boil in water, the fumes are good for colds.

Balsam: Abies Balsamea

Description: A beautiful evergreen which may reach 80' in height but is usually 40' to 60'. Smaller in the Arctic region and the mountains. The bark is gray-brown and nearly smooth but with resinous blisters. The branches are arranged in whorls of 4 to 6 leaves, shiny, dark green, blunt pointed, ½" – 1" long. Cones are 2" – 4" long, purplish, cylindrical, and erect.

Found: Throughout Canada, northern New England states, and west through the Great Lakes states into Iowa.

Use: An antiseptic and healing liquid may be obtained by pricking the amber bubbles on the trunk. The other amber-producing evergreens such as hemlock and the pines may also be used this way. The amber may also be chewed like gum to relieve throat tickle and simple sore throat.

Creosote Bush (Greasewood): Larrea Tridentata

Description: An evergreen shrub with an erect spreading bush which grows to 10' in height. Many short branches, covered with dull green resinous foliage. Solitary yellow flowers in the spring. Spherical fruit is densely hairy. Flowers and fruit may be seen on this plant at the same time.

Found: Southwest United States and Mexico.

Use: An antiseptic lotion is made from a mixture of twigs and leaves in water.

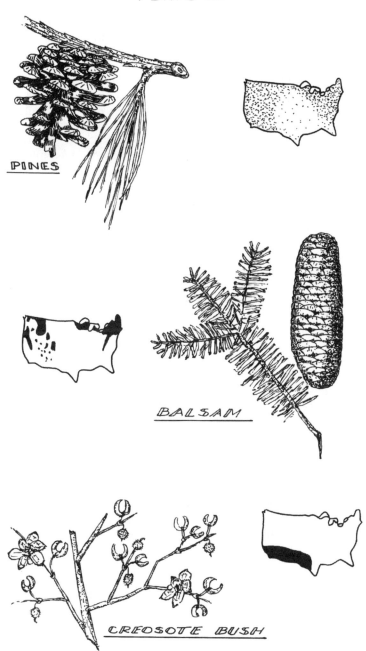

PLATE 25

PINES

BALSAM

CREOSOTE BUSH

PLATE 26

Hemlock: Tsuga Canadenis, Tsuga Carouniana
Description: A forest tree found in rough terrain on rocky ridges, mountain slopes, sides of ravines, etc. Branches are long and slender with slightly drooping branchlets. Twigs are light yellowish brown to reddish brown. Old trees show cracks and ridges covered with thick scales that are red on the underside. Needles are short and flat with a blunt end. Usually in two rows, the needles are bright yellow-green above and silvery below. Needles are ⅓" to ½" long.
Found: Northeastern and northwestern U.S.
Use: As an astringent. Crushed bark and water decoction for cuts, bruises, sprains, and sunburn.

Oak: Many varieties.
Description: Will vary with type.
Found: One or more varieties found over most of the U.S.
Use: As an astringent, boil crushed bark in water.

Sumac: Staghorn (Typhina), smooth (Glabra).
Description: Staghorn: usually a large shrub or a small tree with a rather crooked stem. Branches are coarse. The twigs are pinkish with a velvety feel and appearance. As they mature, they become green and finally smooth and brownish. The bark is dark brown and smooth but rough at old stems. Often cracks into papery scales. The leaves are from 1' – 2' in length and are composed of 11 – 31 sharp-toothed leaflets. Fruit is velvety red in conical clusters. Smooth: similar to the staghorn except for a bluish white coating on the twigs. The bark is lighter and grayer in color. The fruit is much less velvety.
Found: Staghorn sumac ranges through the eastern half of the United States, primarily in the northern states and into the northern area of the southern states. Smooth sumac ranges through the eastern half of the United States and into the west.
Use: Astringent in fruit and bark. Also as a gargle for sore throat. Staghorn fruit boiled in water with sugar added may be used as a lemonade substitute.

Sassafras: Lauraceae
Description: A common tree or shrub in the eastern half of the United States. They show 3 types of leaves: two-lobed mitten-shaped, three-lobed, and no lobes. Fruit turns purple in the fall. Twigs are bright green.
Found: Eastern half of U.S.
Use: A drink made by simmering roots in water is reputed to be of value in many diseases. Represented here only as a mild stimulant and a warming tonic.

PLATE 26

HEMLOCK

OAKS
(MANY VARIETIES)

(BUR OAK)

SUMAC

(STAGHORN)

SASSAFRAS

Jewelweed (Touch Me Not): Impatiens Capensis, Impatiens Biflora

Description: There are 5 known varieties in North America, growing in low moist soil and preferring shade. It may reach a height of 5' although normally less. The plants are annuals with tender, juicy stems which appear almost transparent. Flowers range from white to yellow to orange. The ripe seed pods explode when touched, scattering the seeds. The garden variety Balsamina or Balsam Weed is similar.

Found: Primarily in the eastern half of the United States with several varieties in the far Northwest.

Use: External only. The fresh juice from the succulent stem and leaves is reported to be useful in eliminating the effects of exposure to poison ivy, poison oak, and poison sumac. However, a person's sensitivity to such poisons and the time lapse between exposure and application will undoubtedly be factors in effectiveness. Very often jewelweed will be found growing near poison ivy. Chance or is this an example of one of nature's intended checks and balances? Jewelweed is also useful for insect bites when crushed leaves and stems are applied as a poultice.

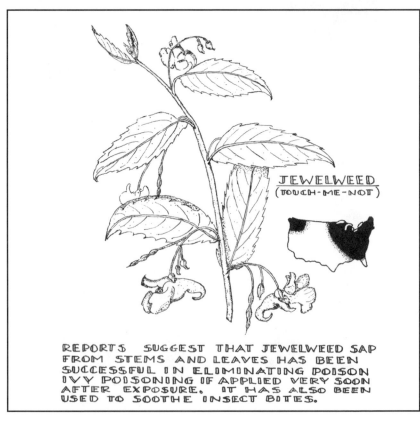

JEWELWEED
(TOUCH-ME-NOT)

REPORTS SUGGEST THAT JEWELWEED SAP FROM STEMS AND LEAVES HAS BEEN SUCCESSFUL IN ELIMINATING POISON IVY POISONING IF APPLIED VERY SOON AFTER EXPOSURE. IT HAS ALSO BEEN USED TO SOOTHE INSECT BITES.

TANNIC ACID

Contrary to what the word "acid" would seem to imply, tannic acid has no irritating or toxic properties. It is an excellent astringent, will harden skin, form a protective coating over superficial wounds, bites, burns, etc., and check bleeding from small wounds. Combined with powdered charcoal (1 part tannic acid to 2 parts charcoal), it constitutes an antidote for many types of swallowed poisons.

As you will note from the preceding discussion of medicinal plants, many contain readily available amounts of tannic acid — witch hazel, hemlock, oak, sumac, and flowering dogwood. The barks of each, crushed and boiled in water, will produce a brown liquid rich in tannic acid.

Application can be accomplished by either sponging on the affected area or by applying on a wet compress.

Unfortunately, many aqueous solutions are unstable over long periods due to bacterial growth and oxidation. As spoilage sets in, one will note an increase in a precipitate in the bottom of the container, a darkening of the liquid, and an increase in objectionable odor.

BASIC FIRST AID REVIEW

Survival medicines as have been discussed will be "hit and miss" regardless of the time one might donate to learning about them. As in other phases of survival, the written word accompanied by a drawing or two tends to greatly oversimplify the difficulties one would encounter in the field.

It is one thing to indicate that a certain bark has excellent astringent properties and another to gather, prepare, and use under survival conditions. We have, at least, discussed the potential uses of specific medicinal plant species and can now only hope that they never will have to be widely used.

In concluding this chapter, there are a number of basic first aid preventions and/or treatments which should be included.

I. Poisoning
   A. External
     1. Skin contamination
       a. Poison ivy
       b. Poison oak
       c. Poison sumac
       d. Buttercup

The degree of susceptibility to skin contamination will vary from person to person. Skin reddens in affected areas with the eventual formation of blisters that itch intensely. The affected areas easily spread by scratching or by clothing irritation.

Wash exposed areas immediately with strong soap, or in the absence of soap, jewelweed if available.

2. Skin burning
   a. Ultra violet ray poisoning
      Keep area covered. Use a tannic acid wash.
B. *Ingested Poisoning*
   There are three basic types of poisoning which one might face within a survival situation.
1. Mushrooms
   There are many examples of poisonous mushrooms given in my 1963 edition of *Wilderness Survival.* I stressed the importance of being absolutely sure of the edibility of a mushroom before using. The amanita mushroom family is the most dangerous of the poisonous types, and the reader should make himself completely aware of the poisonous and edible varieties before using. If you have eaten a poisonous variety, your poisoning will be characterized by acute abdominal pain, diarrhea, vomiting, increase in sweating, and general discomfort. These attacks come in bouts with intervening periods of emission. Without medical assistance, shock and convulsions may result, followed by death.

   Any type of mushroom poisoning should be regarded as serious especially since certain drugs present in mushrooms may cause hallucinations requiring restraint to avoid bodily injury.

   When no professional medical assistance is available, every effort should be made to rid the system of the poison as quickly as possible. Your system is already attempting to carry out this elimination through the actions of vomiting and diarrhea. However, if possible you should prepare an antidote from items which are available to you. A mixture of two parts powdered charcoal to one part tannic acid will be helpful.

   After this mixture is swallowed, it should be allowed to remain in the stomach for four or five minutes and then eliminated by induced vomiting.

   A useable charcoal can be obtained from the sticks in your fire. The best way to obtain it is simply to scrape the charcoal from partially burned twigs, crushing it into as fine a powder as possible. Tannic acid can be obtained as indicated in the section on tannic acid.
2. Poisonous plants
   Repeat process as in number 1
3. Bacterial action on food
   Same as number 1
C. *Injected poisoning*
1. Bees, wasps
   Such stings are painful but normally do not create a serious hazard beyond pain swelling and discomfort. Try a mud pack on the affected area.

2. Spiders

Spider bites can be serious, especially those of the black widow and tarantula. If a bite of a black widow can be identified, treatment similar to a snake bite can be administered.

3. Scorpions

Scorpion stings, although feared, are not normally too serious. The person suffers acute pain and swelling and reddening of the infected area, and in extreme cases the victim may suffer from severe headache, increased flow of saliva, abdominal pain, and nausea.

Keep as quiet as possible and if cold water is available, the affected area could be submerged or repeated cold compresses applied.

4. Snake bites

There are four poisonous varieties of snakes in the United States — moccasins, rattlesnakes, copperheads, and coral. If bitten by a poisonous snake of the first three categories, there will be a distinct puncture and tooth pattern easily distinguished from that of non-poisonous varieties. In the case of the coral snake, after striking, the snake will actually hold onto the victim.

Bites of poisonous snakes are extremely dangerous, and the bite of any of these could prove fatal, especially if no professional medical attention is available. The first emergency measure should be the application of a handkerchief, rope, or stout string above the bite (between the bite and the nearest blood pressure point). This band should not be use as a tourniquet to cut off the blood supply but rather a method for slowing the blood flow.

After the band has been applied, a series of cuts should be made through the puncture area in an attempt to expel the poison via the blood and white corpuscles. As the poison spreads and goes under the band you have applied, it may be necessary to relocate the band and make another series of incisions. Hopefully your wilderness treatment will prove successful. It will also be well to note the importance of lying down and remaining calm as possible. Apply cold packs and if possible submerge the inflamed area. Be sure to keep the area in question as low as possible. Do not elevate.

5. Animal bites and scratches

Animal bites and scratches are included under the section on poisoning. Since any type of animal bite or scratch can very easily become infected, the best suggestion possible for this type of situation would be to cleanse the wound and apply an antiseptic.

II. Heat exhaustion

Heat exhaustion is the inability of the human organism to cope with climatic conditions by ridding the body of excessive heat. This type of exhaustion can be a very unpleasant experience especially under survival circumstances. There is a feeling of complete drain of energy. The face is pale, the temperature is sub-normal, and the skin is wet and clammy. The condition would also be accompanied by severe chills. One should wrap in a blanket and lie down. One should, if available, also take sips of weak salt water and cups of strong coffee or tea. A cup of strong sassafras tea may also be worthwhile.

III. Burns and scalds

It is no longer accepted practice to apply grease or oil to a burn. Under survival conditions the burn or scald should be washed thoroughly after which a tannic acid solution should be applied. In keeping with the best sanitary conditions, the burn or scald should be protection but allowed as much air as possible to speed drying. Sunburn can also be treated with tannic acid by simply sponging a solution on the burned area. It might also be noted that the strawberry is an excellent medication for simple burns. If you are fortunate enough to find wild strawberries, rub the burned surface with the strawberry or in severe cases make a poultice of the crushed berries.

IV. Hysteria

At the beginning of this book, I indicated the extreme importance of staying calm and not allowing oneself to panic. Hysteria results from one's inability to cope with the survival situation. If at any time during your survival experience you feel that you are "losing your grip," take some immediate diversionary action. Scream, throw rocks, take a swim, do anything that you can. Tire yourself out. This should relieve your tension. I must emphasize again the importance of taking immediate action since if you fail to do so, you may not be able later to cope with your situation.

V. Fractures

All we can do is hope that one will be fortunate not to be faced with a fracture of any kind. If one does occur, about the only thing that can be done is to splint the fractured area and bind it tightly enough to minimize movement of the broken bone.

SKIN CONTAMINATES

POISON SUMAC

POISON IVY

POISON OAK

BUTTERCUP

IMPORTANT!

When burning leaves which might contain poison ivy, oak or sumac, stay clear of the smoke. Smoke carries the poison which may be harmful externally and internally!

SALT

Salt is usually sought as a good seasoner and not as often regarded as having medicinal properties except possibly as a gargle for sore throat.

However, if one stops to consider its value as a gargle, its potential as a first aid tool becomes more obvious.

1. **Antiseptic** — Used either in crystalline form sprinkled sparingly in a wound or in a water solution. A hot compress soaked in a solution of 2 or 3 teaspoons of salt boiled in water is good treatment for infections.

2. **Gargle** — Strong solution in warm water.

3. **Heartburn** — Dissolve a few grains on the tongue.

4. **Toothache** — Saturated solution of salt water is placed on a bit of cotton or cloth and put on the tooth.

5. **Laxative** — Dissolve 1 or 2 teaspoons of salt in a glass of water and drink.

6. **Heat exhaustion** — Dissolve small amounts of salt in a glass of water and swallowed slowly.

7. **Sore eyes** — Put a few grains of salt in an ounce of water — preferably boiled — and use as a wash.

8. **Sore mouth** — A gargle solution also is good to swish around in the mouth for sore gums.

9. **Brushing teeth** — Rub on salt with your finger if no brush is available.

Nature does not have a ready source of salt except in various crystalline deposits. The only plant which I could verify as having a high saline content is coltsfoot (Tussilago Farfara).

Coltsfoot is a perennial herb of the compositae family. Its creeping rootstock gives rise to slender flower stalks which reach about 12" in height. The yellow flower heads resemble dandelions in early spring and bloom before the leaves develop. Leaves are orbicular, slightly lobed and toothed, green on the upper side and white beneath.

Take the leaves, roll them into small balls, and let them dry in the sun or set them near a fire where they can be force-dried.

When dry, place the leaf-balls on a hot, flat rock and let them burn away to ashes. The ashes are very saline.

If you have aluminum foil, roll the leaves in small balls, roll in foil and place in hot coals for 10 minutes. Remove from coals, cool, then crush foil ball a number of times between fingers. The fine powder that the ball contains is your salt. By using aluminum foil you can make up a quantity of salt portion to carry with you.

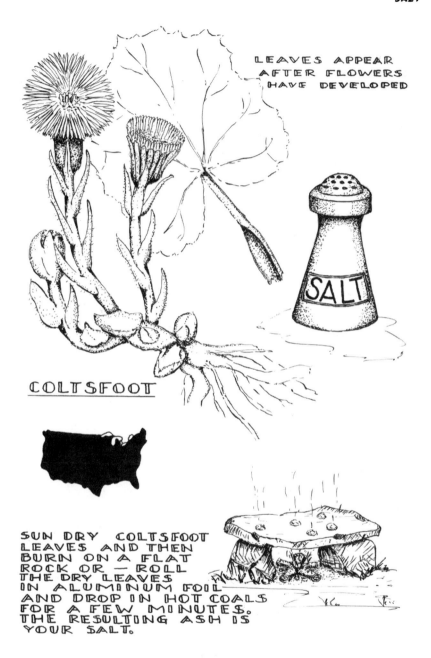

LEAVES APPEAR
AFTER FLOWERS
HAVE DEVELOPED

SALT

COLTSFOOT

SUN DRY COLTSFOOT
LEAVES AND THEN
BURN ON A FLAT
ROCK OR — ROLL
THE DRY LEAVES
IN ALUMINUM FOIL
AND DROP IN HOT COALS
FOR A FEW MINUTES.
THE RESULTING ASH IS
YOUR SALT.

SEE CHAPTER ON MEDICINAL
PLANTS FOR MORE INFORMATION.

97

SOAP

One can regain some semblance of well being — if lost or stranded — but lucky enough to have a bar of soap. Unlikely? Yes! But a real morale booster if available! A dash of cold water in the face is usually satisfactory but my, is it nice to get those grubby paws cleaned up!

A poor variety of soap can be produced by mixing animal fat and wood ashes together with a little water and boiling slowly for a time. The mix won't smell like roses — that I guarantee! But the job it will do is passable.

On your next camping trip, scoop some wood ashes into your greasy frying pan, and add some water. Let this mixture simmer for a few minutes. It won't do a perfect cleanup job but will give you a clue as to what you can do with a little know-how.

If you are lucky enough to be in an area where nature has provided natural soaps, so much the better!

In general terms, soap-bearing plants and trees contain saponins. Saponins dissolve readily in water in clear solutions which froth when shaken. The solution also forms lasting foams when mixed with various oil, and therefore, are called detergents or cleansing agents.

1. Soapbark Tree: Quillaja Saponaria

Cultivated in the southern United States and in California. May grow to a height of 60 feet with shiny ovate leaves 2 inches long, white flowers and winged seeds; the powdered bark is used as soap.

2. Bouncing Bet or Soapwort: Saponaria Officianalis

A stout, smooth perennial of the pink family. Grows 2' to 3' high with many oblong leaves and very dense, flat-topped clusters of white or pink flowers about 1" across. Plant juices form soap.

3. Soapberry tree

Three varieties of this tree are found: Sapinous Saponaria – Florida; Sapinous Marginatus – North Carolina to Florida; Sapinous Drummonoii – Kansas to Louisiana and Arizona

Grows to a height of 20 to 30 feet. Evergreen compound leaves, small white flowers, and small orange-brown, shiny fruit. The bark is light gray and flaky. Crush pulpy fruit and use as soap substitute.

4. Soapbush: Chenopodium California

Native to California. Found in stream beds on moist slopes or in open foot hills. Roots are grated and used as soap.

5. Southern Red Buckeye: Aesculus Pavia

Usually a shrub with smooth bark from gray to brown. Leaflets are 2" to 6" long, usually 5, elliptical to obonate, shiny and fine toothed. The flowers are red. Most common along streams and in woods from Virginia to Missouri and south. Bark contains saponin used as a soap substitute.

The bark also contains esculin, which in a 4% solution, is an ointment good for sunburn since esculin absorbs ultraviolet rays. I have requested further word on this but at the time of writing can report nothing further.

6. Spanish Bayonet: Yucca Filamentosa

A large plant with broad rigid leaves terminating in a sharp, thorny point. Leaves are orientated from base to stalk. The flowers are white and cup-shaped, clustered toward the top of the stem. The fruit is green or yellow. The plant is found on plains, hillsides, and in dry soil with plenty of sunlight in approximately the southern one-half of the United States and into Mexico. Root is washed, peeled, and cut into sections. When agitated in water, a thick soapy foam forms which is a good cleanser and hair shampoo.

SOAP

MAINTENANCE OF HEALTH IS VITAL DURING A SURVIVAL ORDEAL! KEEP CLEAN! ITS A GOOD MORALE BOOSTER TOO!

BOUNCING BET

SOUTHERN RED BUCKEYE

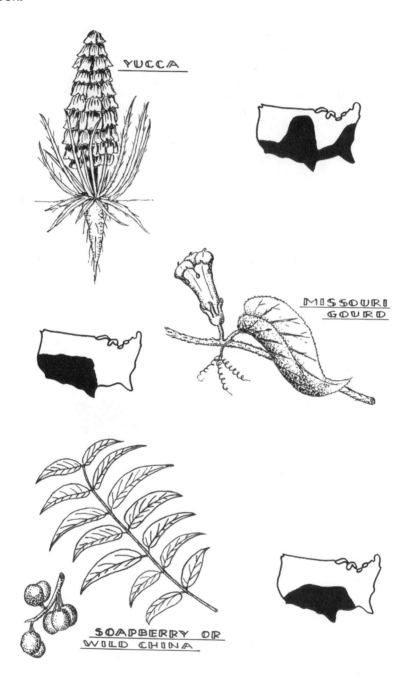

YUCCA

MISSOURI GOURD

SOAPBERRY OR WILD CHINA

FISHING

Under survival conditions, you will find it much easier to sustain life by remaining near water whenever possible.

Plant food is much more prevalent near water. The combination of adequate food and good water will also attract animal life in much greater abundance. Since most authorities agree that there is a greater abundance of food in water than on land, knowing the ins and outs of obtaining food from water is extremely important and worth reviewing.

It would be well to concentrate on methods used in constructing your fishing equipment — fish, hooks, lines, lures, etc. Plates 27 – 30 suggest a few ideas both in the construction of hooks and the addition of lures.

None of the hooks require great skill although patience should be used in fitting the parts together. Also keep in mind that the size of the hook is important. An overall length of between 1" – 1½" should prove to be the best.

With the line you will make, it will be much better to satisfy yourself with the smaller species of fish rather than making any attempt to register a catch. See page 104 for methods of making line.

WHERE, WHEN, AND HOW

Millions of dollars are spent each year on fishing equipment of all kinds. Special baits and lines are in constant demand as are water temperature gauges, fishing almanacs, depth gauges, etc. However, the elusive fish somehow manages not to conform to written rules relative to his capture. One day he is hooked in shallow water with a minnow, the next he becomes a sucker for worms dangled in a deep, quiet pool. Still on other occasions he seems oblivious even to the most succulent grub.

I hesitate adding my suggestions but...

1. Fish in the early morning and early evening near shore.
2. Anytime of the day or night is satisfactory if the water is deep.
3. Fishing just before a storm may be worthwhile although I feel the concept is overworked.
4. Watch for the fish to jump especially if there are a great number of bugs on the water.
5. In unfamiliar territory look for the following signs for best areas to fish:
   a. At the edge of weed beds
   b. Near the fallen trees
   c. Areas full of lily pads
   d. At the base of rapids
   e. Beneath undercut banks

As an added suggestion, ask yourself where you might be if you were a fish. Fish there! You may be surprised at the results.

Use whatever bait is available. A bit of bright cloth, a button, a cray-fish, insects, grasshoppers, grubs, minnows, fish eggs, and worms all deserve your consideration.

Plate 28 shows some additional methods of fishing. The trigger stick is relatively easy to make. I can speak for its effectiveness, having caught carp in this manner. Stand quietly in the water and hold the trigger end down. When a fish appears, move rapidly!

PLATE 27

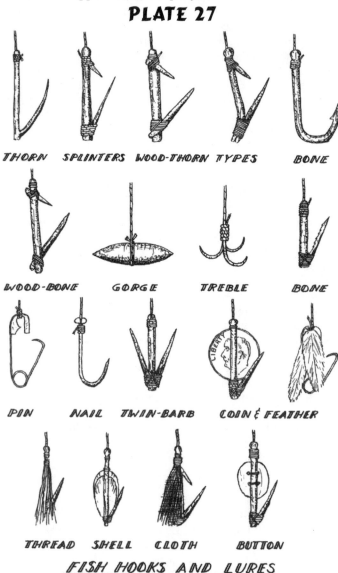

THORN   SPLINTERS   WOOD-THORN TYPES   BONE

WOOD-BONE   GORGE   TREBLE   BONE

PIN   NAIL   TWIN-BARB   COIN & FEATHER

THREAD   SHELL   CLOTH   BUTTON

FISH HOOKS AND LURES

PLATE 28

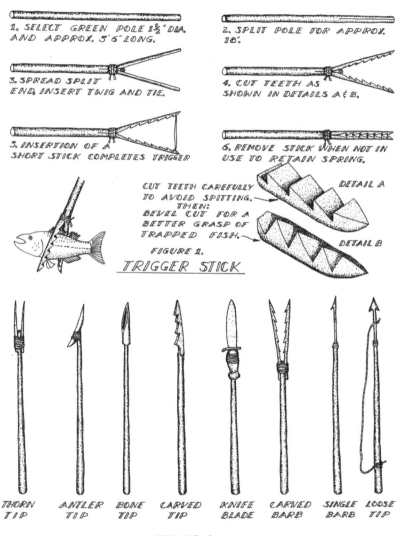

1. SELECT GREEN POLE 1½" DIA. AND APPROX. 5' 6" LONG.

2. SPLIT POLE FOR APPROX. 18".

3. SPREAD SPLIT END, INSERT TWIG AND TIE.

4. CUT TEETH AS SHOWN IN DETAILS A & B.

5. INSERTION OF A SHORT STICK COMPLETES TRIGGER

6. REMOVE STICK WHEN NOT IN USE TO RETAIN SPRING.

CUT TEETH CAREFULLY TO AVOID SPLITTING.
THEN:
BEVEL CUT FOR A BETTER GRASP OF TRAPPED FISH.

DETAIL A

DETAIL B

FIGURE 1.

TRIGGER STICK

THORN TIP · ANTLER TIP · BONE TIP · CARVED TIP · KNIFE BLADE · CARVED BARB · SINGLE BARB · LOOSE TIP

FIGURE 2.

FISHING SPEARS

103

PLATE 29

FISHING LINE

FIGURE 1 INDICATES A TWO STRAND LINE MADE FROM PLANT FIBER. FASTEN THE TWO FIBERS TOGETHER AND SECURE (A.). TWIST INDIVIDUAL FIBERS CLOCKWISE BETWEEN THUMB AND FOREFINGER OF EACH HAND (B.). AT THE SAME TIME, TWIST THEM TOGETHER COUNTERCLOCKWISE (C.)(D.). AS THE FIBERS GROW SHORT ADD ADDITIONAL ONES AS SHOWN (E.). A TWENTY FIVE FOOT LINE CAN EASILY BE MADE IN AN HOUR OR TWO.

REMEMBER THAT TWO STRANDS ARE FOUR TIMES AS STRONG AS A SINGLE ONE. BE PATIENT!

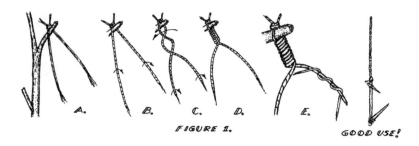

A.   B.   C.   D.   E.

FIGURE 1.

GOOD USE!

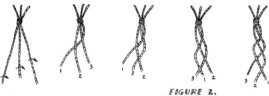

FIGURE 2.

FIGURE 2. DETAILS THE STEPS IN MAKING BRAIDED LINE. PROCEED AS SHOWN IN FIGURE 1. A-B AND THEN BRAID RATHER THAN TWISTING STRANDS.

FIGURE 3.

IF SEVERAL PIECES OF LINE ARE TO BE TIED TOGETHER, FIGURE 3 SUGGESTS A GOOD METHOD. IT SEEMS NOT TO WEAKEN THE LINE AT THE KNOT WHICH IS OFTEN THE CASE.

SOURCES OF FIBER

1. STINGING NETTLE — PROTECT YOUR HANDS! SOAK THE DRY STALKS, ROLL AND REMOVE OUTER SKIN. FIBERS STRONGER THAN HEMP OR COTTON. 2. THISTLE — INNER FIBER. 3. WILLOW — INNER BARK. 4. BASSWOOD — INNER BARK. 6. GRAPEVINE — BARK. 7. HICKORY — BARK. 8. RED CEDAR — INNER BARK. 9. OSAGE ORANGE — INNER BARK.

PLATE 30

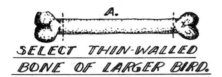

SELECT THIN-WALLED
BONE OF LARGER BIRD.

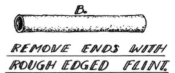

REMOVE ENDS WITH
ROUGH EDGED FLINT.

SPLIT AND CUT
INTO SECTIONS.

DRILL SERIES OF
HOLES. SAW OR CUT
TO ENLARGE HOLE.

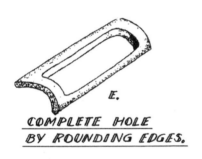

COMPLETE HOLE
BY ROUNDING EDGES.

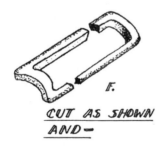

CUT AS SHOWN
AND —

COMPLETE

IROQUOIS FISH HOOK

UTENSILS & TOOLS

MATERIALS AND METHODS

The drawings shown in Plate 31 are a few ideas worth trying when you are in need of eating utensils. These can all be made from wilderness materials.

A good sharp knife will be helpful in most cases but not absolutely essential for all. A clam shell, rubbed clean with sand, will also make a very useable all-purpose utensil.

The only statement which might be made in regards to the bark spoon and ladles is the types of bark best used in construction. Willow, birch, or aspen bark will work about equally well providing that they are soaked for a day or two in order to give them ample elasticity. Careful use of canoe birch may allow you to make a vessel immediately. Plate 32 shows two types of bark vessels which can also be constructed from native materials. The diagrams are self-explanatory; be sure and soak the bark before use for best results.

A number of methods which may be used in cooking foods are discussed on page 110. At various times throughout the years, I have utilized all of the methods shown. Some methods work better than others, or one will be more to your liking than another.

STONE TOOLS

The construction of stone tools discussed in detail on pages 111 – 115, is one phase of survival which, to my knowledge, has never been extensively covered. While a student of archaeology in Arizona, I had many opportunities to examine stone tools and to try my hand at making some of the more simple items. Actually, once the fundamentals are mastered, crude but useable tools can be made with a minimum of effort. The best types of stone to use are flints and cherts. Obsidian, a volcanic glass, may also be used although it is not native to all areas. These stones will break with a conchoidal fracture which produces a very sharp edge.

PERCUSSION FLAKING
FOR ROUGH SHAPING

After locating a useable stone, break off sections and select a piece that has possibilities. Hold it either between your thumb and the first two fingers or in the palm of your hand holding it in place with your four fingers. Since the flakes are very sharp, it is suggested that you place a heavy cloth or a piece of leather in the palm of your hand or over your thumb. See pages 114 – 115 for step-by-step explanation of this process.

The best flaking tool is the last 5 or 6

inches of a deer antler. A piece of hard wood or a nail will also work, but not as well. Take the flaking tool in your right hand and press down on the lower edge of the stone to be flaked. This pressure will force small flakes to break off. Repeat this process along the edge until a row of flakes has been removed. Remove a second row of flakes by pressing on the new sharp edge which you have created. Keep in mind that the pressure angle will control the length of the flake removed. A short pressure angle will remove a short flake, a long pressure angle will remove a

PRESSURE FLAKING

APPLY PRESSURE TO SHARP EDGE OF STONE. USE ANTLER OR EQUAL.

long flake. When you have removed several rows of flakes from one edge of your stone, turn it over and repeat the same process on the other side. A little experimentation will show you the best way to proceed.

After you have practiced a few simple shapes, try your hand at making a stone drill or a knife blade. You may be surprised at the results you attain.

There are other implements which also can be made from stone. If you are near a stream containing water-washed boulders, you should have very little trouble in locating shapes which will lend themselves to crude axe-heads or mauls. Other uses of stone are mentioned elsewhere in this book.

USING CLAY

If you are near water, attempt to find a bed of clay. If successful, try your hand at making pottery. Although clay is not easy to find in all areas and may vary in useability, you may pass a lot of hours trying your hand at simple vessel forms. A basic form can be molded by simply taking a ball of clay, kneading it, adding water enough to make it workable, and mixing in small amounts of sand, shell or grass to minimize cracking during drying.

Press your thumb into the center of the ball and then slowly pinch the clay between your thumb and finger. Eventually, this pinching action will thin the walls of your vessel to ¼ inch or less. Smooth the surface with water and allow to dry slowly for several days. When the vessel is not cold to the touch, place it on a flat stone and kindle a fire around and over it. Heat until your vessel is red hot and maintain for a few minutes and then slowly let the fire die down, allowing the vessel to cool naturally. When cool, tap the rim lightly with your fingernail. If it rings, your first vessel is a success! If it has a dull metallic clank, either it has not been fired long enough or it is cracked.

During any wilderness ordeal it is important to stay active and alert. Finding things to do is important, especially if you decide to stay put for a few days to prepare for future moves. Every successful project using nature's offerings builds your confidence. As you gain confidence, you improve morale. As you grow to understand and use the things around you, the more naturally you will be able to cope with your situation.

PLATE 31

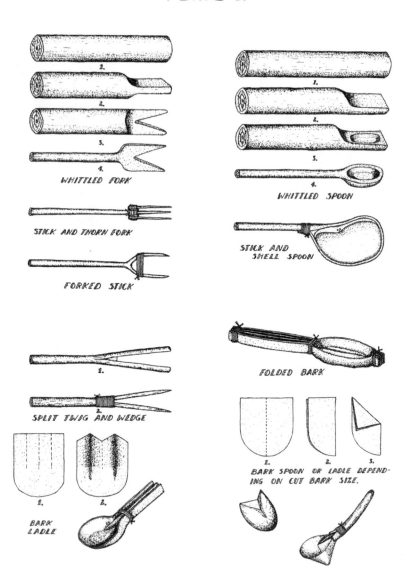

WHITTLED FORK

WHITTLED SPOON

STICK AND THORN FORK

STICK AND
SHELL SPOON

FORKED STICK

SPLIT TWIG AND WEDGE

FOLDED BARK

BARK
LADLE

BARK SPOON OR LADLE DEPEND-
ING ON CUT BARK SIZE.

PLATE 32

TYPE 1.

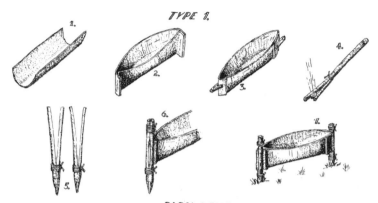

BARK VESSEL

1. SELECT YOUR BARK - WILLOW, BIRCH OR ASPEN ARE BEST - AND CUT 10-18 INCH STRIP 6 TO 7 INCHES IN DIA. 2. FOLD ENDS 3. PEG ENDS TEMPORARILY. 4. DROP BURNING HOT PITCH ON SEAMS. 5. CUT STAKES AND PREPARE AS SHOWN. 6. INSERT BARK. 7. COMPLETE AND READY FOR USE.

TYPE 2.

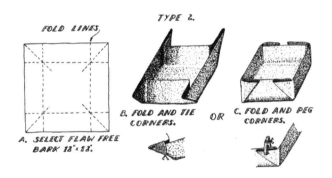

FOLD LINES

A. SELECT FLAW FREE BARK 18" x 18".

B. FOLD AND TIE CORNERS.   OR   C. FOLD AND PEG CORNERS.

WHEN CONSTRUCTING A BARK VESSEL, IT IS SUGGESTED THAT THE BARK BE SOAKED FOR AT LEAST 24 HOURS PRIOR TO USE.

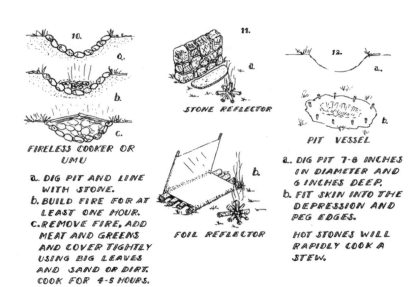

10.
a.
b.
c.

FIRELESS COOKER OR UMU

a. DIG PIT AND LINE WITH STONE.
b. BUILD FIRE FOR AT LEAST ONE HOUR.
c. REMOVE FIRE, ADD MEAT AND GREENS AND COVER TIGHTLY USING BIG LEAVES AND SAND OR DIRT. COOK FOR 4-5 HOURS.

11.
a.

STONE REFLECTOR

b.

FOIL REFLECTOR

12.
a.
b.

PIT VESSEL

a. DIG PIT 7-8 INCHES IN DIAMETER AND 6 INCHES DEEP.
b. FIT SKIN INTO THE DEPRESSION AND PEG EDGES.

HOT STONES WILL RAPIDLY COOK A STEW.

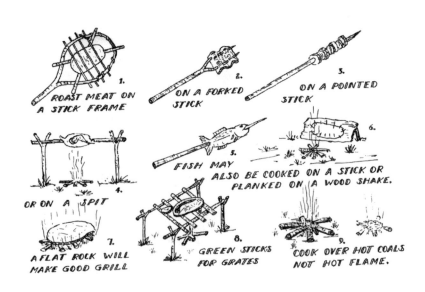

1. ROAST MEAT ON A STICK FRAME

2. ON A FORKED STICK

3. ON A POINTED STICK

4. OR ON A SPIT

5. FISH MAY

6.

ALSO BE COOKED ON A STICK OR PLANKED ON A WOOD SHAKE.

7. A FLAT ROCK WILL MAKE GOOD GRILL

8. GREEN STICKS FOR GRATES

9. COOK OVER HOT COALS NOT HOT FLAME.

PREHISTORIC STONE TOOLS

One has only to visit a museum almost anywhere in the world to realize the important part stone played in the everyday life of prehistoric man.

Since he was forced to use most of his energy collecting food, finding shelter, and protecting himself, he used natural materials close at hand to help make his life as easy as possible. Since stone was usually abundant and easy to use, it became a natural choice. He used it in making stone shelters, grinding edible seeds, making his weapons, and constructing a variety of tools.

Shown on pages 112 and 113 along with their modern counterparts are a group of the most common types of prehistoric tools made from chipped stone. Under survival conditions, stone tools may be important to you.

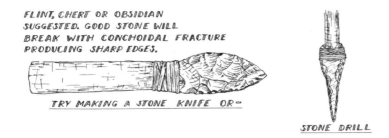

FLINT, CHERT OR OBSIDIAN SUGGESTED. GOOD STONE WILL BREAK WITH CONCHOIDAL FRACTURE PRODUCING SHARP EDGES.

TRY MAKING A STONE KNIFE OR—

STONE DRILL

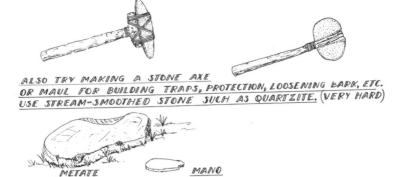

ALSO TRY MAKING A STONE AXE OR MAUL FOR BUILDING TRAPS, PROTECTION, LOOSENING BARK, ETC. USE STREAM-SMOOTHED STONE SUCH AS QUARTZITE. (VERY HARD)

METATE   MANO

OTHER USES MAY ALSO BE FOUND FOR STONE. A METATE OR GRINDING STONE TOGETHER WITH A MANO OR HAND STONE MAY BE USED TO GRIND GRAINS, SEEDS, ETC.
STONE MAY ALSO BE USED IN FIRELESS COOKING, IN MAKING OVENS, REFLECTORS AND FOR USES MENTIONED ELSEWHERE.

111

SCRAPER

AXE

MAUL

KNIFE

DRILL

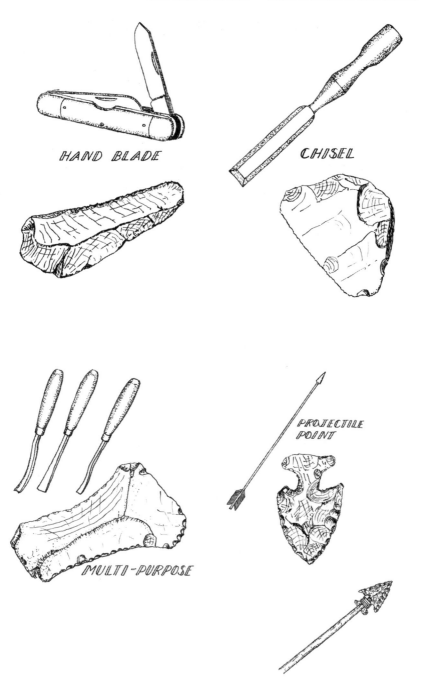

HAND BLADE

CHISEL

MULTI-PURPOSE

PROJECTILE POINT

THE ART OF STONE CHIPPING

Selecting the types of stone most suitable for tool making may present some problems. Only certain types are satisfactory and even the proper varieties may be impure or grainy and therefore unsatisfactory.

Flint, chert, and obsidian are the best. However, quartzite, jasper, chalcedony, rhyolite, and basalt may be used with good results.

A stone in order to be useable must break with a conchoidal (con-coy-dal) fracture. This means that the flakes produced by chipping will resemble the outside form of a clam or oyster shell. When you have obtained what you believe to be the proper type, strike it sharply along the edges and examine the chipped surfaces. If you have produced chipped surfaces that are roughly like the depressions and elevations of a shell, you are ready to proceed (Figure 1).

I strongly recommend that if you practice at home you wear gloves and safety glasses. Small chips can be dangerous since they may fly quite a distance. The chips are also extremely sharp and may produce many tiny cuts in the fingers and hand.

FIG. 1

Practice striking off some large chips which you think could be made into a tool of some kind. Don't be discouraged if it takes a while to get the hang of it (Figure 2).

If you prefer, you may strike off chips as shown in Figure 3. If you decide on this method, place a piece of leather or a cloth pad in the palm of your hand under the stone you are chipping. Avoid bruising or cutting your palm as you strike the stones together.

FIG. 3

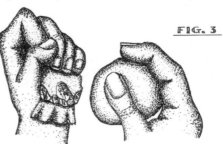

FIG. 2

When you have completed the rough shaping of your tool, you are ready to start the finished shaping as shown in Figure 4. Commence by striking a series of chips one after another along the edge. When the first row has been completed, repeat the same process along the other edges. When this has been completed, you may go back over the other surfaces to complete the rough shaping as necessary.

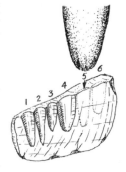
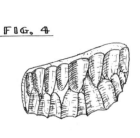

FIG. 4

The type of chipping used so far is called *percussion chipping*. It has been accomplished by striking one stone against another. In the final steps, you will use some percussion chipping but will primarily rely on *pressure flaking*. As the term suggests, pressure flaking is accomplished by applying pressure to your stone to force off chips. Deer antler makes an excellent pressure flaking tool. An entire antler tip (Figure 5) or a small tip securely fastened to a strong wood shaft is the very best (Figure 6). If no antler is available, a blunt pointed hardwood stick or a nail may be used but should be considered inferior.

FIG. 5

FIG. 6

Pressure flaking is accomplished as shown in Figure 7 with pressure applied to the sharp edge of the flint. By pulling the flaking tool toward you as shown by the arrow, flakes will pop off. With practice you will be able to control their size.

In conclusion, let me say that it is important for you not to be discouraged if you don't have perfect luck the first time. Keep practicing. Adapt the procedures to fit your likes or dislikes and your facility with the required skills.

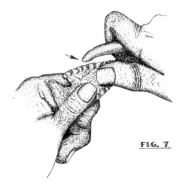

FIG. 7

PROTECTING YOUR FEET

"City fellas" without shoes are about as useless as wet matches. An overturned canoe may create a swimming problem that eventually finds you on shore without shoes. Accidentally blundering into a knee-deep quagmire may also cost you your shoes. Rodents have also been known to drag off a shoe or two while the owner sleeps peacefully.

Regardless of the circumstances, a few hours of sharp pine needles, stinging nettles, burdock, sharp rocks, and toe-catching roots will convince even the strong at heart that some sort of foot gear is essential!

There are a number of alternatives from which to choose. The general situation will help in the decision. If you still have your socks, fill them half-full of moss or cattail down and then force your feet into the remaining room. Eventually the filling will shift and will necessitate readjustment and eventually the sole of the sock will probably fall apart. A slab of green bark will also work for awhile as will a cloth pad made from your shirt or pants.

As detailed in Plate 33, a more permanent type of sandal requires some time and patience to make. A few alternatives in construction are also listed. If you feel that the results do not justify the time, stop and realize that a battered pair of feet will compound your survival ordeal by limiting your mobility.

PLATE 33

GRASS, PLANT FIBRE, OR LEATHER STRIP SANDALS —

1.

COLLECT YOUR PLANT
FIBRE OR COMMERCIAL
TWINE.

2.

OR

MAKE YOUR
NEEDLE FROM
BONE OR THORN.

3.

MAKE A NEEDLE
FROM SHARP POINT OF
YUCCA LEAF. THE
ATTATCHED LEAF
FIBRES ARE THE
TWINE.

4. CONSTRCTION MATERIAL MAY INCLUDE BUNDLES OF GRASS,
NETTLE OR BARK FIBRE, BRAIDED SKIN OR CLOTH, ETC.

5. TIE YOUR FIBRES EVERY
1⅛ INCHES WITH A
CLOVE HITCH.
SOAK BEFORE USING.

TYING NOT NECESSARY
6. WITH BRAIDED MATERIAL.

7.

ROLL YOUR PREPARED
CONSTRUCTION MATERIAL.
SEW AS SHOWN.

8.

INCREASE UNTIL PROPER
FOOT SIZE IS REACHED.

9.

AFTER ADDING STRAPS, YOUR SANDALS
ARE READY TO GO. REMEMBER THAT WELL
CONSTRUCTED PAIR WILL LAST LONGER. SRH

117

QUICKSAND

Quicksand is not a type of sand but rather a condition created by the combination of water and sand. It can be a deadly troublemaker but its pitfalls can be avoided if one understands the properties that make this sand and water combination hazardous.

Artesian springs bubbling up from below in sandy areas tend to keep the sand particles in suspension. As a result, an area of sand although appearing to be solid may in fact be only semi-solid and unable to support the weight of a hiker or fisherman.

Quicksand is not a concern in flat, waterless areas. Sand needs water to become quicksand. Therefore, hikers and fishermen should be especially wary of streams bordered by bluffs, especially if springs can be seen along the base line of the bluffs. Precautions should also be taken if walking along what appears to be a dry stream bed, along streams, and sandy shore lines. It should also be noted that sand, solid at one time, may be quicksand at other times.

A walking stick should be a basic requirement for hikers with a special use as a probe to test for possible areas of quicksand, remembering that sand that appears dry on the surface may not be solid below.

Quicksand has taken many lives as a result of panic generated by misinformation which has suggested that once in quicksand, one will slowly and surely be sucked down to suffocation. Quicksand has greater density than water and can support more weight, allowing one to lie back with arms outstretched and float while slowly working backwards towards solid ground. In some instances the quicksand may be solid enough to allow one to roll through it or run across it. Whatever the method used, first rid yourself of as much extra weight as possible, stay calm, rest occasionally as you work, and of course, call for help if assistance is nearby. Remember that moving too rapidly may cause vacuum pockets around your body which can pull you under. Quicksand victims are those that fight it!

TRAPS & SNARES

Although you may be able to exist by foraging for wild plant foods, meat will give you the best possible source of protein and concentrated nutrition. In most cases, animals are also much easier to prepare and do not require cooking containers. An animal may also supply you with fur, sinew, and bone which we recognize as playing an important part in construction of other survival equipment. Although some animals and birds may not be as tasty as others, most are edible.

In order to trap or snare animals, it is necessary to know when, where, and how to best accomplish your goals. Some of the general rules to remember are: 1) In areas inhabited by animals, you will be able to note signs of their presence. Look for tracks, trails, dens, runways, marks where they have feed, etc. 2) Animal traits and tracks are easily discernible in the woods and since many animals are creatures of habit, you can expect that these trails will be used time and time again. 3) Animals and birds will congregate in areas where good food and water supplies are available. 4) It is much easier to locate animals by sitting quietly and observing the terrain than by charging through it. By sitting quietly for a few minutes, you may be able to observe a great number of types of animals and birds that you might not have seen otherwise. You may also be able to locate birds' nests much easier in this way. 5) Most animals are more normally seen in the early morning and the early evening rather than during the day.

Snares and traps fall generally into four categories: 1) The fixed snare; 2) The unbaited hanging snare; 3) The baited hanging snare; and 4) The deadfall trap. Your choice of the proper type will depend upon the availability of materials and the type of animal you are attempting to catch.

For example, a fixed snare would be a wise choice if attempting to catch rabbits. It should be set across a rabbit run with the noose approximately 4" in diameter with the bottom not more than 3" above the ground. The rabbit will run into the snare head first and since he will not generally reverse his direction, the noose will continue to draw tighter as he fights to get through. Unbaited hanging snares will also work well for rabbits (Plate 34).

A noosing wand will be effective if you have the patience to sit quietly for an hour or so. Lay the noose over the opening in an animal burrow or den. Pull the noose closed as soon as the head of the animal appears in the right position.

The baited snares shown in Plate 35 are self-explanatory as to method of construction. As the animal eats the bait, he disengages the lever, and the sapling snaps up, closing the noose.

The deadfalls shown in Plate 36 are all baited. As the animal eats the food, the trip mechanism is disengaged, causing a heavy log or stone to fall on the trapped animal.

Spring-set fishing equipment may also be constructed. The top diagram on page 123 details a simple method that works quite well. When the fish takes the hook, it disengages the trigger causing the sapling to snap up, pulling the fish out of the water. In using this method, do not have too much spring. Too strong a spring will pull the hook from the fish's mouth or worse yet, toss your dinner halfway across the lake.

The fish trap, requires a good deal of ingenuity in construction but is exceedingly effective. If you are establishing a semi-permanent camp near water, construction may be worthwhile if this trap is used for nothing more than a live box.

PLATE 34

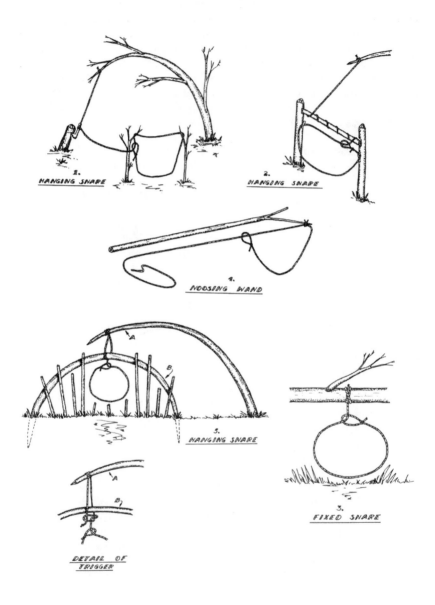

1.
HANGING SNARE

2.
HANGING SNARE

4.
NOOSING WAND

5.
HANGING SNARE

DETAIL OF
TRIGGER

3.
FIXED SNARE

PLATE 35

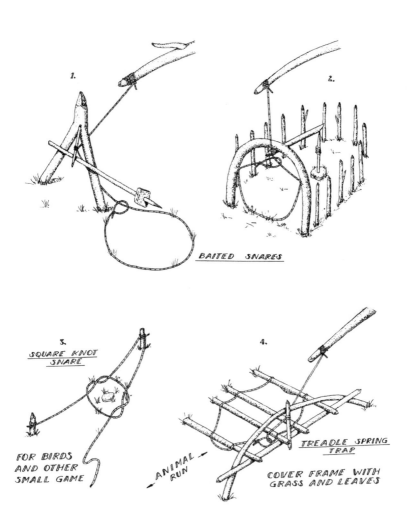

1.

2.

BAITED SNARES

3.
SQUARE KNOT
SNARE

4.

FOR BIRDS
AND OTHER
SMALL GAME

ANIMAL
RUN

TREADLE SPRING
TRAP

COVER FRAME WITH
GRASS AND LEAVES

PLATE 36

DEADFALL

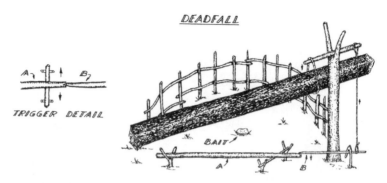

A   B

TRIGGER DETAIL

BAIT

A   B

NOTE ON DEADFALLS

RATHER THAN BAIT THE DEADFALL
IT MAY PROVE MORE PRACTICAL
TO CONSTRUCT IT AT THE MOUTH
OF AN ANIMAL DEN — THE TRIGGER
BEING SPRUNG MANUALLY.

AN ANIMAL STEPPING
ACROSS "A" WILL DIS-ENGAGE
"B" CAUSING LOG TO FALL.

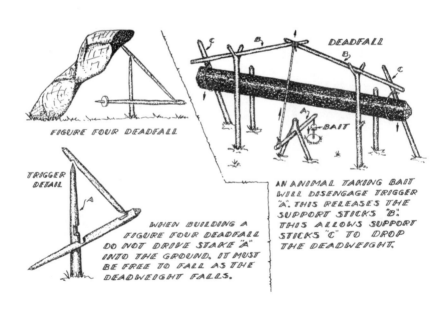

FIGURE FOUR DEADFALL

DEADFALL

BAIT

TRIGGER
DETAIL

WHEN BUILDING A
FIGURE FOUR DEADFALL
DO NOT DRIVE STAKE "A"
INTO THE GROUND. IT MUST
BE FREE TO FALL AS THE
DEADWEIGHT FALLS.

AN ANIMAL TAKING BAIT
WILL DISENGAGE TRIGGER
"A". THIS RELEASES THE
SUPPORT STICKS "B".
THIS ALLOWS SUPPORT
STICKS "C" TO DROP
THE DEADWEIGHT.

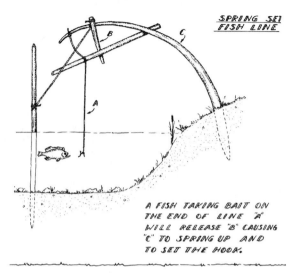

SPRING SET
FISH LINE

A FISH TAKING BAIT ON
THE END OF LINE "A"
WILL RELEASE "B" CAUSING
"C" TO SPRING UP AND
TO SET THE HOOK.

DIP NET

AN EMERGENCY DIP NET MAY BE
CONSTRUCTED BY SPLITTING A BRANCH
AS SHOWN (DETAIL A). THEN—

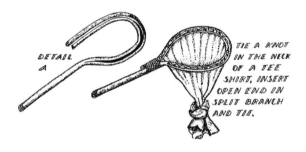

DETAIL
A

TIE A KNOT
IN THE NECK
OF A TEE
SHIRT, INSERT
OPEN END IN
SPLIT BRANCH
AND TIE.

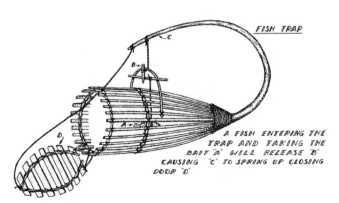

FISH TRAP

A FISH ENTERING THE
TRAP AND TAKING THE
BAIT "A" WILL RELEASE "B"
CAUSING "C" TO SPRING UP CLOSING
DOOR "D".

WEATHER

In most social gatherings, light conversation will more than likely include some discussion of the weather. Weather means many things to many people depending on what their particular desires might be at the time.

To the family preparing for a picnic, sun and warmth are important while at the same time farmers may be hoping to relieve the dry conditions with plenty of rain. To the skier, ample snow is of prime importance, while for the road department, heavy snow means additonal work.

To the person involved in a survival situation, weather is also of prime importance. If one needs water, he will hope for rain. If he must travel long distances, he will probably hope for clear, rather cool conditions. At night he will hope for temperatures that will keep him relatively comfortable and warm. Obviously the longer one is faced with a survival ordeal, the more important weather becomes. Since it represents a phenomenon over which a person has no control, the best one can do is prepare for it in the best possible way.

Rather than discuss the technical aspects of weather — why and how it happens, it would seem most logical to mention conditions which might prevail at a given time and a given place and under specific circumstances in hopes that the reader will use the knowledge to his best advantage.

Based on many years of recorded data, there are a number of combined facts which may be expected to produce certain climatic results. However, this does not necessarily mean that such situations will produce predictable results 100% of the time, although it does present a highly reliable basis for prediction.

I. Fair Weather
1. Cumulus clouds are seen dotting the sky in all directions.
2. A light breeze prevails from the west or northwest.
3. If there is an early morning fog, it is usually burned off by noon showing predominately blue sky.

II. Bad Weather
1. A thickening of cirrus clouds indicates the possibility of the coming of bad weather.
2. The light fluffy cumulus clouds bunch up and develop into larger masses vertically (cumulonimbus).
3. The sky to the west grows dark.
4. A prevailing north wind shifts rather rapidly in a counter-clockwise direction from north, to west, to south.
5. Southerly winds increase noticeably in velocity.

III. Clearing Weather
1. Low clouds rise to higher elevations. Winds change direction, particularly east winds shift to the west.

IV. Falling Temperatures
1. Southerly winds shift towards north.
2. Night skies are bright and crystal clear.

V. Rising Temperatures
1. Temperatures will remain steady or rise if the weather remains cloudy.

GAUGING TEMPERATURE

Humidity plays an important part in earth temperature and obviously a knowledge of humidity will help the person in a survival situation to prepare accordingly. High humidity will keep the earth's temperature more uniform, since heat from the surface will be reflected back to earth from moisture particles in the air. The lower the humidity, the less reflection occurs and the more the earth's surface is allowed to cool. Much the same situation will occur at night, depending upon the degree of cloud cover. The clearer sky during the night, the less reflection and hence the greater the temperature drop. A cloudy sky at night will most always guarantee less surface temperature decline.

Applying these principles of humidity and temperature, one can conclude that these general conditions can be expected.

1. Woodlands will be warmer in winter than open country.
2. Wind speeds in forest lands will be lower normally than those in open country.
3. Relative humidity will be higher in forested areas than in open areas.
4. The average daily temperature range in valleys will be greater than in hilly areas.
5. Wind velocity range from high to low will not be as great in valleys as in hilly areas.
6. Fog will be more predominant in valleys than in the hills.
7. Frost will be more prevalent in low areas than in high.

WEATHER LORE

Most of us have at one time or another attempted to predict the weather. Presuming that we have no scientific reports available, our conclusions on what the day might bring may very possibly be based on weather sayings which have been around since the beginning of time.

For example, "A red sky in the morning is a sailor's warning; a red sky at night is a sailor's delight," or "A ring around the moon means rain."

Both sayings have some validity. In the case of the former, I have seen a rainy day result from a red sky in the morning but am inclined to think that it is more than likely a case of being in the right place at the right time.

However, a ring around the moon has considerably more validity — being an accurate method of prediction in from 50 – 75% of the time.

Long-time residents of specific areas may also have locally believed methods of weather forecasting. In such cases, years of exposure to given sets of circumstances build up knowledge, allowing for high degrees of valid conclusions.

More subtly, change in barometric pressure may cause some people discomfort, such as head or body ache — not very scientific, but reliable to a degree at least!

Whatever the situation, we must accept whatever weather appears and learn to live with it as best we can.

WINTER SURVIVAL

Some years ago I received a copy of *Jack London's Stories for Boys* and have always remembered one particular story titled "To Build a Fire." It is appropriate reading for anyone venturing out in subzero weather since it vividly describes the tragic misadventures of a greenhorn under such conditions.

Under the best conditions, being lost or stranded during the winter months will compound the problems one must face to stay alive and well. A person properly clothed and equipped with a basic understanding of problems that may arise can be relatively comfortable. Since the chances of supplementing your clothing are nil, food, shelter, and warmth must of necessity receive your full attention.

Although general conditions may cause alterations in your plans, kindling a fire should be the first consideration in most instances. A crackling fire will afford not only needed warmth but will also go far in boosting your morale. At 30° below zero, there are few things more important. Naturally in cases of high wind and heavy snow, a windbreak should be constructed first as a precautionary measure. In order to fully appreciate the impact of winter survival methods, I suggest that everyone read Jack London's story.

During the summer months when the temperature is in the 80s, it is not too difficult to bring wood to its kindling temperature of between 800° – 900° Fahrenheit, depending on the type of wood being used. It is also much easier to determine the dryness of wood during the summer months. Kindling a fire at 30° below zero requires you to raise the temperature at least an additional 100° in order to reach the same kindling point. A wood fire at 30° below will also be harder to rekindle once it burns down.

Difficulties may also be encountered in making a fire by flint and steel for the reason mentioned above. The same conditions will exist when attempting to make fire by friction. For best possible results, select your fuel carefully from above the snow level. If such fuel is not readily available, remove the bark for fuel below snow line and scrape the frost or ice from wood without bark. When possible, split the wood open, exposing the drier inner areas. As an added suggestion, stock an adequate supply of extra wood close by so that it may be dried and warmed somewhat. A reflector fire is by far the best for all around winter use. If properly constructed and used, it can be an invaluable asset.

Whenever I plan on being out in the woods in winter for any extended period, I carry a 4" length of candle wrapped in good-sized piece of heavy duty aluminum foil. A candle will give off a surprising amount of heat to warm your hands and will warm up a cup of snow for drinking. It will also afford welcome light for your shelter or snow house. A little wax rubbed on small twigs will also be helpful in getting your fire started.

If no candle is available, carry a piece of paraffin wrapped in foil. You can build a makeshift candle by cutting off a ¾" square, punching a small hole through the center and inserting a wick made of some bits of braided cloth, a short section of shoestring, etc.

WINTER SHELTERS

Winter shelters may be constructed along the same lines as those suggested for summer use. The addition of packed snow over the top and/or sides will allow you to make a very cozy retreat. Whenever possible, a pine bough, dry leaf, or dry moss floor should be added as insulation against the frozen ground. In very deep snow, dig a burrow. It will be quite liveable, noticeably warmer, and natural protection against cold winds.

With ingenuity and patience you may also construct a snow house. Firmly packed snow that can be cut into blocks is a prerequisite. Construction methods are also important since a hasty job may make the entire structure collapse before you are half done.

In building any type shelter, check the wind direction carefully and build so that the open end is away from the prevailing wind. This will give you maximum protection from the wind and minimize the smoke problem.

FOOD FORAGING

Finding food will be a serious problem at best. Plant food will be difficult to locate and may be restricted to a few dry berries, possibly a nut or two, rose hips or the inner bark of trees. However, there are some possibilities of locating dry plant stalks which may lead you to edible roots and tubers. Be certain of their identity.

If near water, you may be able to dig cattail tubers or locate a spring that will yield watercress or other edible plants.

Barring the discovery of a cache of "Quick Frozen Garden Vegetables," trapping and snaring animals will afford you the most reliable source of food. Snow will define trails and runs. By following them you may be able to locate dens, burrows, feeding areas, and possibly even fresh running water.

If a frozen lake or stream is located nearby, you may wish to try your luck at fishing. A button or a bit of bright-colored cloth may be used as bait. If you are lucky enough to locate a cocoon, tear it open use the pupa. You may also find some pupae beneath the bark of trees. Your spear and/or trigger stick may also prove useful in fishing, catching mice, or other small game. If using a trigger stick or spear in ice fishing, dangle a piece of bait in the hole to attract attention. If fishing at night, lay several slabs of bark on the ice near the hole and build a fire. Fish, or even a beaver, may be attracted to the hole by the light.

Turtles burrow into the mud during the winter. If you are able to break the ice over swampy areas, do so and probe around for a turtle. You may come up with a meal or two.

Meat and fish storage is no problem in below freezing temperatures although carnivorous animals may steal your stores if not properly protected.

WINTER TRACKS

RABBIT SQUIRREL FOX RACCOON DEER GROUSE PHEASANT

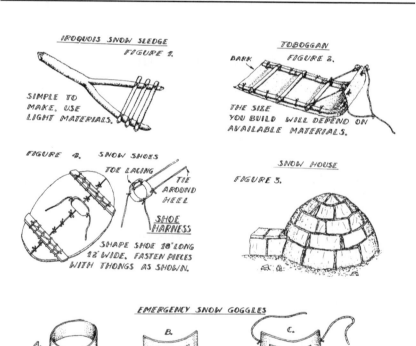

IROQUOIS SNOW SLEDGE FIGURE 1.
SIMPLE TO MAKE. USE LIGHT MATERIALS.

TOBOGGAN FIGURE 2.
BARK
THE SIZE YOU BUILD WILL DEPEND ON AVAILABLE MATERIALS.

FIGURE 4. SNOW SHOES
TOE LACING
TIE AROUND HEEL
SHOE HARNESS
SHAPE SHOE 28" LONG 12" WIDE. FASTEN PIECES WITH THONGS AS SHOWN.

SNOW HOUSE FIGURE 3.

EMERGENCY SNOW GOGGLES
A. B. C.
A. CUT BARK STRIP SUCH AS BIRCH. B. CUT SECTION TO FIT ACROSS FACE AND MARK NOSE AND EYE LOCATIONS. C. CUT AND ADD THE STRAPS. GOGGLES ARE ESSENTIAL FOR LONG DAYS IN BRIGHT SNOW.

PERSONAL PROTECTION & TRAVEL

EYE PROTECTION

Anyone who has ever had the experience of spending a day in snow country in bright sun will agree, without sunglasses the experience can be a very unpleasant one. To a lost or stranded person attempting to travel in snow, some sort of eye protection becomes increasingly important as time goes on. Without some eye protection, snow blindness may be the ultimate result. Although not necessarily a permanent condition, snow blindness may completely incapacitate a person for many days and hence make survival nearly impossible.

Snow blindness is an inflammation of the underside of the eyelids. The condition, which may range from simple inflammation to total blindness for varying periods depending on the length of exposure, is caused by constant exposure to the reflection of the sun on snow. First signs of inflammation are manifest by a feeling of sand in the eyes. As the situation grows more acute, pain increases.

If the first signs appear, they can be eliminated or alleviated noticeably in a number of ways. If one has access to charcoal, quantities should be rubbed into the eyelids, cheeks, and on the bridge of the nose to reduce glare on the eyes.

Snow goggles can forestall or eliminate the possibility of blindness depending upon the care with which they are made. In principle, the goggles cut down the amount of light which reaches the eye. This noticeable reduction in the light which reaches the eye allows it to react normally. Goggles will restrict the field of vision since the slits are only approximately ⅛" wide and 1" long. Once you have become accustomed to this restricted vision, it will cause no serious problem. Emergency snow goggles can be made from a strip of smooth bark 2" wide cut from a tree 4" – 6" in diameter. Measure the location of your nose and the approximate location of your eyes and make cuts accordingly. A strip of cloth or bark may be used to fasten the goggles in position. Your eyelashes may cause some discomfort, but by cutting a 2" strip vertically from a small sapling, a pair of goggles can be made that will be concave enough over the eye area to minimize the problems with eyelashes. If you are lucky enough to have a good knife, a pair of wooden goggles with interior eye depressions can be made. I can speak for their reliability.

If one is wearing regular glasses, pieces of adhesive tape may be placed over the lenses, leaving narrow slits in the center.

Whatever the equipment one possesses, it is reasonable that one will find some method of eliminating the dangerous glare. If total blindness occurs, the eyes should be covered with a dark bandage for a day or two.

129

SNOWSHOES

Travel in deep snow without proper equipment is impossible for more than a few short minutes. The exertion required in making such travel attempts may result in serious physical problems. It is therefore recommended that any thought of travel in snow be ruled out unless one has or can put together a pair of snowshoes. An emergency pair can be constructed with simple materials and a little patience.

Walking on snowshoes is not difficult to learn although you may end up head first in a snowbank until you get the drift of things. You must learn to walk with your legs wider apart than normally. If you do not, one snowshoe will overlap the other and cause you to fall. With a little patience, you can learn to walk rapidly and even to run.

Snowshoes fall into two general design categories — the tailed variety for travel in flat, open country and the bear paw type for travel in woodlands and hilly terrain. Plates 37 and 38 illustrate both types.

Fragile, poorly made snowshoes may suffer from serious ailments. The frame may break and webbing may sag. As a result, the user may be subjected to unnatural body stresses resulting in painful leg and back strains. Whatever the situation, it is well worth the time and effort to make the snowshoes you have as serviceable as possible — and to keep them that way!

Tailed snowshoes should be at least 42" long and 12" wide for a person weighing between 125 and 172 pounds. For a person weighing above 175 pounds, the length should be increased to 48" with a width of approximately 14". The tailed snowshoe may be flat although often the front edge is curved up about 2" or more.

The bear paw snowshoe should be approximately 20" long and 13" wide for a person weighing up to 175 pounds. Above 175 pounds, the length should be increased to approximately 30" long and 15" wide.

Snowshoes of these dimensions may be difficult to build from natural materials. However, for best results keep as close to the given dimensions as possible.

As mentioned earlier, damaged or poorly constructed snowshoes can create serious muscular problems. With this in mind, there are several basic thoughts that should be followed in order to minimize damage. First of all, hard shoe or boot heels will cause rapid deterioration of snowshoe strings. For this reason no-heeled shoes or boots are by far the best. If one plans extended snowshoe travel and has only boots with heels, it is suggested that some tough and pliable material such as leather or canvas be fastened under the heel to minimize string damage. If possible, the heel could be removed from the boot.

Secondly, snowshoe strings must be kept taut! When a pair is ready for use, one may judge whether or not the strings are taut enough by standing on them in snow flat-footed and rocking back and forth slightly. If your weight depresses the strings enough at the heel to tend to let you fall over backwards, the strings are too loose. A properly strung snow-shoe will tend to keep your boot sole parallel with the snowshoe frame.

Learning to walk on snowshoes is not difficult, and the procedure can be mastered in about an hour although until one is accustomed he will suffer from muscle aches. In learning to walk it is essential that the center of gravity be such that when the snowshoe is attached to one's boot and a step is taken, the back of the snowshoe will drag on the snow. If this does not occur, the toe hole in the snowshoe and/or the boot straps must be adjusted forward.

In walking it is essential that the snowshoe remain paralled with the surface of the snow. In order to accomplish this, the user must walk flat-footed. If either the toe or heel of the snowshoe sinks into the snow, one will become aware that he is not walking properly.

If one is forced to construct a pair of emergency snowshoes, it will be well worth his effort not to hurry. A simple type of emergency snowshoe can be made by filling an old shirt with dry grass or leaves as shown in Plate 37. The second type, requiring more labor, may be built with two forked sticks placed end to end interwoven. Cross members and webbing are added. The method shown at the top of Plate 38 also utilizes two forked sticks with framing and webbing added. If thin slabs of wood are available, they may be fastened together and utlized as shown in Figure 4 of Plate 38. Other framing ideas are shown in Figure 5 of Plate 38.

Let me say again that excellent improvised snowshoes can be built, providing one applies himself to the task. At a recent Boy Scout winter camporee, I saw a number of homemade snowshoes used in racing con-tests over rugged terrain. Although some types disintegrated immediately, most held up and showed the care taken in their construction.

SLEDS

Plate 39 shows three types of improvised sleds that can be con-structed from material at hand (see also Figures 1 and 2 on page 128). As in the case of the snowshoes, it is well worth the extra time spent to do a good job of contruction. The sled size should be based on the amount of equipment one has to carry but keep the size as small as practical. As a rule of thumb, the size of the sled runner surface should be at least equal to the size of the snowshoe one is wearing. However, if one is operating in hilly country with opportunities to use the sled as a toboggan, the size should be adjusted. The sled should never become a burdensome piece of equipment.

PLATE 37

Emergency
Snowshoes

EMERGENCY SNOWSHOE MADE BY FILLING A SHIRT WITH GRASS OR LEAVES.

FASTEN SNOWSHOE TO YOUR BOOT WITH THE SLEEVES.

FIGURE 1.

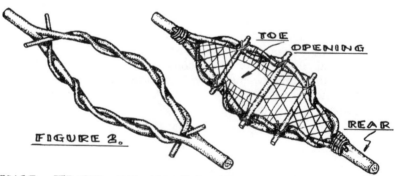

FIGURE 2.

TOE
OPENING

REAR

THIS TYPE OF EMERGENCY SNOWSHOE CONSTRUCTED OF TWO INTERWOVEN FORKED STICKS WITH FRAME AND MESH.

PLATE 38

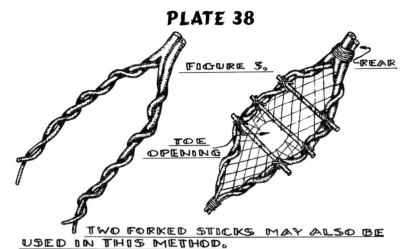

FIGURE 3.

REAR

TOE OPENING

TWO FORKED STICKS MAY ALSO BE USED IN THIS METHOD.

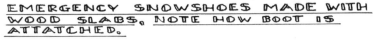

FIGURE 4.

EMERGENCY SNOWSHOES MADE WITH WOOD SLABS. NOTE HOW BOOT IS ATTATCHED.

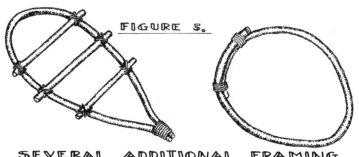

FIGURE 5.

SEVERAL ADDITIONAL FRAMING IDEAS.

PLATE 39

Emergency Sleds

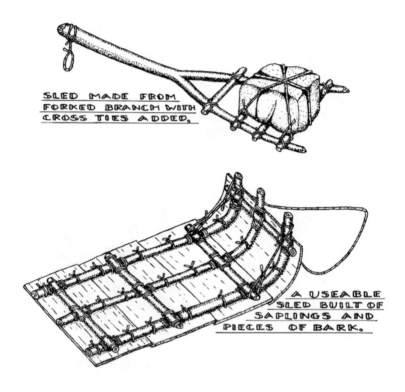

SLED MADE FROM FORKED BRANCH WITH CROSS TIES ADDED.

A USEABLE SLED BUILT OF SAPLINGS AND PIECES OF BARK.

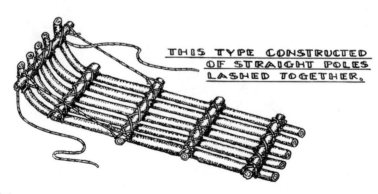

THIS TYPE CONSTRUCTED OF STRAIGHT POLES LASHED TOGETHER.

CLOTHING

Clothing or lack of it will always be a problem, especially in extremely cold weather. Eskimos have proven that many thicknesses of heavy clothing are not necessarily the secret to keeping warm and comfortable. An Eskimo wears a single outer garment of skin with the fur side in. This layer of fur creates a dead air space which acts as a very fine insulator. Modern insulated underwear is based on the same principle. In order to maintain the dead air layer, air circulation must remain at a minimum. For that reason, it is essential that your clothing be closed around the ankles, waist, wrists, and neck. Constant circulation of air in your clothing will minimize the effectiveness of the dead air layer.

Perspiration is also a menace since it dampens clothing. Damp clothing conducts heat from the body and reduces the air space which is acting as the insulating layer. If you become overheated, open your clothing from time to time.

As a final note, remember that hands and feet cool much faster than the body proper. Guard against frostbitten and frozen fingers and toes by keeping them as warm and dry as possible.

HYPOTHERMIA

Hypothermia is a simple ailment but quite deadly if not recognized for its potential danger and if early symptoms are ignored. Some years ago I was ice fishing on a Wisconsin lake in January. Although I thought I was dressed properly, an incessant wind brought my temperature down and fortunately activated a danger signal which made me head for shore. For every two steps forward on the ice, the wind blew me back one. I eventually made it to the car and warmth and realized how dangerous my situation had been.

Hypothermia is regarded as unquestionably the greatest hazard facing hikers. It has taken the lives of many who failed to understand the dangers inherent in hypothermia and the need to recognize the warning signals.

Physiologically when chilled, a hiker's autonomic nervous system attempts to restore heat by tensing the muscles and causing the person to shiver. The problem is compounded if the hiker is tired, hungry, and wet.

As the body attempts to conserve heat, the blood vessels contract which reduces the flow of blood to the skin and extremities. The central nervous system goes amuck, the body loses even more heat, the temperature plummets. When the body temperature falls below normal, the mind becomes confused. Respiration and heart rates slow and unconsciousness follows. Death may occur quickly when body temperature drops to about 78°.

Most cases of hypothermia may be avoided if one uses common sense. Don't attempt to outguess Mother Nature! If lost, you should hole up and keep warm and dry. Those who respect questionable weather conditions will probably live to do it again which is far better than the alternative!

If confronted with someone who seems to have symptoms of hypothermia and is still conscious, get them out of the wind and out of wet clothes. If available, feed them high energy foods and warm liquids. Get them into a sleeping bag with another person to share body heat. If the victim is unconscious, a warm bath will help the thawing process.

135

AN OUNCE OF PREVENTION

Very few campers, hikers, hunters and fishermen are familiar with survival kits; even fewer carry one. A kit regarded as non-essential until needed, suddenly becomes invaluable.

Most of us are cursed with a sense of false security that tells us "it couldn't happen to me." As a result, proper precaution is often overlooked.

While in a wilderness area, a survival kit should be required equipment. It should not be too large or too heavy to become burdensome and yet should be large enough to hold those items of an essential nature.

Review the subjects covered in previous chapters and compile a list of those items that would be easier to carry than to improvise in the field. Since a survival kit must be compact, include only items that could be packed in a container approximately 3" wide, 4" high and 1½" deep. Naturally, you must eliminate plans for including an air mattress, tent, stove, helicopter kit, etc.

SURVIVAL KIT

1. Halazone tablets
2. Aluminum foil (12" x 24") folded into a 3" x 4" pad
3. Fishing equipment
    a. 2 small sinkers
    b. 1 trout fly
    c. 6 miscellaneous hooks
    d. 1 small treble hook line with spinner
    e. 1 artificial worm with hook
    f. 50' 15 lb. fish line (also many other uses)
    g. 25' 10 lb. nylon line (also many other uses)
4. Surplus Air Force survival compass (less than 1" in diameter)
5. Small magnifying glass
6. Sewing needles (larger sizes)
7. Small 2 blade pocket knife
8. Small plastic container of a mixture of salt and pepper
9. Small plastic container of saccharin
10. Flexible saw blade (can be rolled up)
11. 6 first-aid adhesive bandages
12. Iodine for first aid (also water purification)
13. Razor blade
14. Leather cord
15. Stainless steel signal mirror 3" x 4"
16. Pencil
17. Small pad of paper
18. Sheet of plastic, 6' x 8' (strap to outside of kit)
19. Pack of few individual containers of powdered coffee and a few bouillon cubes in extra spaces
20. Matches waterproofed with paraffin

A surplus U.S. Army first aid kit with belt fasteners works well!

I suggest that the kit be worn on your pants belt so that it will be with you as long as you are clothed. In most instances even if your canoe should be overturned, you would get to shore without losing your pants. As a further suggestion, all of the items should be in watertight containers, such as plastic pill bottles sealed with masking tape. The case itself should be securely closed to keep you from utilizing the equipment except in true emergency situations.

ADDITIONAL READING

Boy Scouts of America *Scout Field Book,* New Brunswick, N.J., 1948.

___ *Explorer Manual,* 1955.

___ *Handbook for Boys,* 1917.

___ *Handbook for Boys,* 1938.

___ *Winter Camping,* 1927.

Collier's Encyclopedia — Various references.

Fernald, M.L. & A.C. Kinsey. *Edible Wild Plants of Eastern North America,* Harper & Brothers, N.Y., 1958.

Gilcraft. *Preparing The Way,* C. Arthur Pearson Ltd., London, 1935.

Marshall, Nina. *The Mushroom Book,* Doubleday, Page & Co.

Mathews, Ferdinand Schuyler. *Field Book of American Wild Flowers,* Revised and enlarged by Norman Taylor, G.P. Putnam & Sons, N.Y., 1955.

Medsger, Oliver Perry. *Edible Wild Plants,* The MacMillan Co., N.Y., 1939.

Muenshcer, Walter Conrad. *Poisonous Plants of the United States,* The MacMillan Co., N.Y., 1951.

Seton, Ernest Thompson. *The Book of Woodcraft,* Garden City Publishing Co., N.Y., 1921.

Smithsonian Institution, Bureau of American Ethnology. *Handbook of South American Indians,* Vols. I – IV, 1946 – 1949.

United States Naval Training Institute. *How To Survive On Land and Sea,* Annapolis, Md., 1945.

SURVIVOR SELF-QUIZ

1. What is ground water?
2. How do you construct a noosing wand?
3. What part of the Solomons Seal is edible?
4. What is an umu?
5. Name some good types of tinder.
6. List some uses of a leather cord in survival.
7. Where is the water hemlock most commonly found?
8. What is a trigger stick and how is it used?
9. Name 3 edible roots.
10. What is a hand hold?
11. Is the morel mushroom edible?
12. How do you clear & purify water?
13. List a use of cattail.
14. How many types of forks can you make?
15. What is pressure flaking? Why is it useful?
16. List items to include in survival kit.
17. How do you construct fish hooks from 3 types of material?
18. Why is it unadvisable to eat snow?
19. How is thatching accomplished?
20. What weed offers the best fiber for making string?
21. Name and identify three poisonous plants.
22. What are the advantages of a reflector fire?
23. Name two sugar substitutes.
24. What illnesses may be caused from drinking polluted water?
25. What is meant by planking?
26. What is chicory?
27. Describe a method of locating the North Star.
28. Name a use for charcoal.
29. What is a metate?
30. Locate North by using the sun and your watch.

INDEX

INDEX

INDEX

INDEX

INDEX

INDEX

INDEX

INDEX

INDEX

INDEX

INDEX

INDEX

INDEX

INDEX

INDEX

INDEX

INDEX

INDEX

INDEX

INDEX

INDEX

INDEX

INDEX

INDEX

INDEX

INDEX

INDEX

INDEX

INDEX

INDEX

G
Gorge Hook 102
Grapevine 15, 104
Grass 22
Groundnut 47, 60, 64
Grubs 102

H
Halazone ....18 – 19, 137
Hanging Snares ......119 – 121
Hawthorn ....62 – 64
Hemlock 91
Hickory 104
Hypothermia 136

I
Ice Fishing 130
Iodine ....18 – 19, 136

J
Jack-in-the-pulpit 46, 60, 64
Jewelweed ....90 – 91
Jimson Weed 67, 69
Joshua Tree 46, 59, 64
Junipers ....63 – 64

K
Knife, care & use ....24 – 31

L
Landmarks ....7, 9 – 11
Larkspur ....67 – 68
Lean-to ....21 – 22
Leaves ....20 – 23, 64
Lost ....6 – 7, 9 – 11

M
Mano (Hand Stone) 111
Maps 7
Marsh Marigold 42, 52, 64
Matches ....38 – 39
May Apple 43, 52, 64
Milkweed 67, 69
Monkshood ....68 – 69
Morale ....9 – 11
Mushrooms ....70 – 76, 92

M
Mustard 43, 52, 64

N
Needles 117, 136
Nettles 44, 55, 64, 104
Noosing Wand ....120 – 121
Nut Grass 47, 61, 64

O
Oak ....62 – 64, 88 – 89, 91
Onion (Wild) 45, 57, 64
Orientation ....7 – 9
Osage Orange 104

P
Pemmican 65
Pinon ....62 – 64
Plantain 43, 53, 64
Plum ....62 – 64
Poisonous Substances 66 – 69, 71 – 72, 75 – 76
  Plants ....66 – 69
  Mushrooms ....71 – 72, 75 – 76
Pokeweed 43, 53, 64
Prairie Turnip 47, 60, 64
Puffball 70, 72, 74
Purslane 43, 53, 64

R
Rabbits 120
Raspberry 45, 57, 64
Reflector Fire 110
Roasting 110
Roots 64

S
Salt ....96 – 97
Sandals ....116 – 117
Seeds 64
Service Berry ....63 – 64
Set Line 36
Sheaths, knife ....24 – 25
Sheep Sorrel 43, 54, 64
Shelters ....20 – 23
  Brush 21
  Cave 21

140

Remembering my friend, Stan Hamper
By Dick Judd, Jr.

My introduction to Stan Hamper was through the Boy Scouts of Southwestern Michigan. Stan was not only a Boy Scout but a fellow Eagle Scout, and I found we shared many common interests.

During the early 1960s, Richard Gamble, Boy Scout district executive, Stan Hamper, camping event chairman, and I as camping chairman collaborated on outdoor activities for the young Scouts. At that time, our Potawatomie Boy Scout District stretched from Sister Lakes to Vandalia and brought together boys and leaders from both city and farm from all over Cass County.

Stan generated a myriad of great ideas, and it fell to Dick Gamble and me to whittle down the list of activities to what was feasible, considering we were working totally with volunteer help. Of all Stan's ideas, by far the most memorable was introduced at the Fall Camporee of 1965. Stan felt we should instruct the young Scouts in survival techniques such as how to construct shelters and beds in the wilderness, the use of snares and traps, corn grinding, wilderness eating utensils, and identification of edible wild plants. The planning and execution of this activity was great fun, but far and away nothing surpassed the event's *piece de resistance* — the Great Chicken Episode!

My father, Richard Judd, Sr., had an interest in a chicken business which raised 3-day old chickens to laying age in 20 weeks. The males were sorted out at hatching. However, out of the 20,000 chickens of each flock, 80 to 100 males always survived. At 20 weeks these surviving males were separated and either given away or destroyed. It seemed like the ultimate survival exercise to turn loose some 100 male chickens at our campground, located on Lime Lake off Monkey Run Street near Vandalia.

Thus, the stage was set. On Friday night Stan gave the boys instructions on how to trap and snare, properly kill, pluck, and clean, and ultimately cook their "wild game." The training continued on Saturday and finally in the afternoon, the pickup load of 100 rangy male chickens arrived. At the appointed time, Stan signaled their release. No one in the Potawatomie Boy Scout District, boys or leaders, could have predicted what was to follow.

Chickens, boys, and feathers were going in all directions. It was tough to tell what was louder, the shrieks of the boys or squawks of the terrified chickens. Some of the chickens took flight away from the young campers, and others tried to outrun the boys on the ground. Some were tackled, some were struck with large rocks and sticks. Knives and hatchets were thrown until the leaders stepped in to tone down the mayhem.

The killing process was too gruesome to relate in detail except suffice it to say, those who met a swift stroke of the axe were the lucky ones. Feathers were everywhere, and then the cooking process began. Some birds were boiled whole, and some were literally barbequed beyond recognition. The farm boys from Vandalia fared much better than the city boys from Dowagiac. After the cooking preparation the boys sat down to savor their culinary delight, all with big smiles of satisfaction.

Following the campout, Stan and the committee did a critique on the survival campout and came to several conclusions.

1. We were thankful that the most serious injuries to the campers were sprained ankles, scrapes and bruises, and severe indigestion.

2. There are, no doubt, descendants of those chickens running around that woods yet today.

3. It was a great idea, and the chicken episode surpassed anything we had ever done.

4. We would never do it again!

Although never to be repeated, we all agreed that this was one of Stan Hamper's greatest accomplishments.

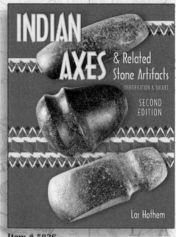